Elite • 155

Roman Battle Tactics
109 BC–AD 313

Ross Cowan • Illustrated by Adam Hook

Consultant editor Martin Windrow

First published in Great Britain in 2007 by Osprey Publishing,
Midland House, West Way, Botley, Oxford OX2 0PH, UK
443 Park Avenue South, New York, NY 10016, USA

Email: **info@ospreypublishing.com**

ISBN 978 1 84603 184 7

Editor: Martin Windrow
Page layouts by Ken Vail Graphic Design, Cambridge, UK
Typeset in Helvetica Neue and ITC New Baskerville
Index by Glyn Sutcliffe
Originated by PPS Grasmere, Leeds, UK
Printed in China through World Print Ltd.

07 08 09 10 11   10 9 8 7 6 5 4 3 2 1

A CIP catalogue record for this book
is available from the British Library

FOR A CATALOGUE OF ALL BOOKS PUBLISHED BY OSPREY MILITARY AND
AVIATION PLEASE CONTACT:

North America:
Osprey Direct
2427 Bond Street, University Park, IL 60466, USA
Email: **info@ospreydirect.com**

All other regions:
Osprey Direct UK
PO Box 140, Wellingborough, Northants, NN8 2FA, UK
Email: **info@ospreydirect.co.uk**

Buy online at **www.ospreypublishing.com**

Acknowledgements

The author would like to thank the Cowan family, Jim
Bowers, Duncan B.Campbell, Lawrence Keppie, Thomas
McGrory, Jasper Oorthuys, Philip Rance, Steven D. P.
Richardson, Robert Vermaat and Martin Windrow.

Quotations from ancient sources are adapted from the Loeb
Classical Library.

Artist's note

Locations of battle sites mentioned in text		
Ancient name	*Modern name/location*	
Adrianople	Edirne, European Turkey	
Amanus, Mt	Mt Amanus, Turkey	
Andretium	Gornji Muc, Croatia	
Aquae Sextiae	Aix-en-Provence, France	
Bibracte/ Helvetii	Mont Beuvray, France. The battle against	
	the Helvetii was fought at Armecy,	
	nr Toulon	
Carrhae	Harran, Turkey	
Chaeronea	Chaironeia, Greece	
Cirta	Constantine, Algeria	
Cremona	Cremona, Italy	
Ctesiphon	c.20 miles SE of Baghdad, Iraq	
Daphne	c.5 miles S of Antakya, Turkey	
Dyrrhachium	Durrës, Albania	
Emona	Ljubljana, Slovenia	
Forum Gallorum	Castelfranco Emelia, nr Modena, Italy	
Gindarus, Mt	Genderesse, Syria	
Idistaviso	? somewhere on course of R.Weser,	
	Germany	
Ilerda	Lleida, Spain	
Issus/Cilician Gates	Iskenderun, Turkey	
Lauron	Lliria, Spain	
Lugdunum	Lyon, France	
Mons Graupius	? Bennachie, Aberdeenshire, Scotland	
	is the favoured location	
Munda	c.5 miles NE of Osuna, Spain	
Muthul, River	Oued Mellag, N of Le Kef, Tunisia	
Nicopolis	Pürk, Turkey	
Nisibis	Nusaybin, Turkey	
Orchomenus	Orchomenos, Turkey	
Pharsalus	Farsala, Greecve	
Philippi	nr Kavala, Greece	
Phraata	nr Hashtrud, Iran	
Pistoria	Pistoia, Italy	
Rhyndacus, River	R.Rhyndacus, Turkey	
Ruspina	Monastir, Tunisia	
Sabis, River	? either R.Sambre or R.Selle,	
	in NW France and S.Belgium	
Saguntum	Sagunto, Spain	
Segovia	Segovia, Spain	
Thapsus	Ras Dimas, Tunisia	
Tigranocerta	Silvan, Turkey	
Uzitta	a few miles SW of Monastir, Tunisia	
Vercellae	Vercelli, Italy	
Vetera	Birten, Germany	
Zela	Zile, Turkey	

ROMAN BATTLE TACTICS 109 BC–AD 313

INTRODUCTION

The study of Roman battle tactics has been likened to crossing a minefield. Doubt has been cast over previous attempts to reconstruct the 'battle mechanics' of the cohortal legion – the principal Roman unit of our period – because its size and organization, command structure and methods of deployment are imperfectly understood (Speidel 1992, 6; Wheeler 1998, 649). This book will focus on the tactics of the legion, because that is the formation for which we possess the most evidence, especially the legions of the Late Republic. The tactics of the auxiliary infantry cohorts and cavalry *alae* of the Empire will be considered where appropriate.

The time span of this book has been chosen to reflect the period in which the cohortal legion dominated the Roman battlefield. In 109 BC the last vestiges of the manipular legion can be discerned in the battle fought between Metellus and Jugurtha by the River Muthul; and AD 313 saw what was perhaps last great encounter of legion against legion (or at least of legionary 'vexillations' – detachments of one or two cohorts) near Adrianople. Soon after this date the legion was greatly reduced in size and status by the army reforms of the emperor Constantine. There are few detailed literary accounts of the legions of the late 3rd and early 4th centuries AD in action; but the evidence of inscriptions indicates the continuity of traditional centurial and cohortal organization, and we can assume that many of the tactics and manoeuvres carried out by the legions of Julius Caesar (our principal source for such matters) were still practiced.

During the 4th century AD the formation that had conquered the Roman Empire, and had successfully defended it for centuries, was whittled down to a unit of c.400 men. The reasons for this decline are outlined in my *Imperial Roman Legionary, AD 161–284* (Osprey *Warrior* series 72). Yet even in this reduced form the legion lived on until the 7th century AD. When the Muslims invaded Syria and Egypt in the 630s and 640s, the Roman armies that met them at Yarmuk, Heliopolis and Babylon (Cairo) were composed, in part, of legions or units descended from them.

Legionaries of the 1st century AD in battle, from a column base in the legionary headquarters building at Mainz, Germany. Note the typical sword-fighting stance of the leading legionary, while his comrade – still holding a *pilum* – lifts his shield to block a blow or intercept a missile. (Photo Jasper Oorthuys)

The size and organization of the legion

The size of legions varied considerably. The preferred number of soldiers in the legion of the Late Republic (the period c.133–31 BC) was 5,000 to 6,000, the latter being an optimum figure and probably seldom realized (Serv. *Aen.* 7.247). During the course of an extended war the effective fighting strength of a legion would fall dramatically. In 54 BC Julius Caesar marched with two legions to relieve the camp of Quintus Cicero, which was besieged by the Nervii, with two legions that totalled 7,000 men (Caes. *BG* 5.49). At the battle of Pharsalus in 48 BC Caesar's legions were even more reduced: having fought through the Ilerda and Dyrrhachium campaigns, the average strength of a legion was 2,750 men. The legions of the opposing Pompeian army were each about 4,000 strong (Caes. *BC* 3.88–89). Following Pharsalus, Caesar pursued the fugitive Pompey to Egypt with two legions, but their combined strength amounted to only 3,200 men (Caes. *BC* 3.106). One of the legions was the Sixth, recruited by Caesar in 52 BC; it suffered yet more casualties in Egypt, and arrived at the battlefield of Zela in Pontus (47 BC) with less than a thousand men (Anon. *BAlex.* 69). If *legio VI* had been raised with a strength of c.5,000, it had lost more than 80 per cent of its effectives in six years of campaigning.

The legions that Mark Antony took to Parthia in 36 BC, including a replenished Sixth (which by then bore the title *Ferrata* – 'Ironclad'), had an average strength of 3,750 each (Plut. *Ant* 37.3). In that year, however, the legions of Lepidus were only 'half full', so with c.2,500 to 3,000 men per legion, and potentially even fewer if they were only half the strength of the fuller legions of the period, i.e. those approaching 4,000 effectives (Vell. Pat. 2.80.1). The two legions with which Lucullus won his great victory at Tigranocerta (69 BC) were each a little over 4,000 strong – powerful units by the standards of the day (Plut. *Luc.* 27.2).

The Imperial legion had a paper strength of about 5,000 soldiers, but again, actual numbers were often far below this. During the early stages of the Illryian Revolt (AD 6–9) the Twentieth Legion was at only half strength when it won a striking victory against 20,000 of the enemy (Vell. Pat. 2.112.2).

What we can say with certainty of the legions of both periods is that they were divided into ten cohorts, and that each cohort was made up of six centuries divided between three maniples (cf Aul. Gell. NA 16.4.6).[1] In the Early Imperial legion the century numbered 80 men, divided into ten *contubernia* (Hyg. *De. Mut. Castr.* 1). The eight soldiers of a *contubernium* formed a mess and tent group, and it has been suggested that they would form a file in the battle line, but there is no ancient evidence to confirm this.

The manipular legion

The legion that preceded the cohortal formation was composed of 30 maniples and divided into three battle lines each of ten maniples. The first and second battle lines – the *hastati* ('spearmen', although by now they fought with heavy javelins called *pila*), and *principes* ('best men') – were organized into maniples each of 120 or 160 men. The *triarii* ('third line men') – veterans equipped with thrusting spears – were always organized in maniples of 60 men. Each maniple was officered by

---

[1] Cf = compare with

two centurions (*centurio* – 'commander of 100'), one senior and one junior. The senior centurion was in overall command, but in battle the control of the left side of the maniple was delegated to the junior, who would assume complete command if the senior was incapacitated or killed. As well as two centurions, the maniple had two *optiones* to keep order at the rear of the maniple, and two standard-bearers (*signiferi*) (Polyb. 6.21–25).

The maniple would also have had at least one trumpeter. The standards provided a visual focus for advance or retreat; the trumpet provided audible signals and relayed commands from the general's trumpeters to the standard-bearers. Despite the duplication of officers and 'NCOs' (this term is convenient, though not really appropriate for the Roman army), the maniple was not divided tactically into two centuries: it was a single fighting unit. Polybius emphasizes that the pairing of officers was so that the maniple would never be without a leader.

Readers should also note that the manipular legion did not have a commander in the modern sense. Its six tribunes were men of extensive military experience and were far superior in rank to the centurions, but they did not have specific command functions (the same was true of legionary tribunes during the Empire). The only officers with clear command and tactical responsibility were the centurions (Isaac 1995, 23–24). Our instinctive need to interpret ancient organizations and ranks in familiar modern terms is often an obstacle to understanding; our distinctions between field and company officers, warrant officers and non-commissioned officers simply have no direct Roman equivalents. The essential fact seems to be that the legion was an organizational entity rather than a strictly 'pyramidal' fighting unit. It deployed in three mutually supporting lines, and its size might suggest a parallel with a modern brigade, but this resemblance is more deceptive than helpful. That the manipular legion functioned perfectly well without a commander indicates thorough standardized training, throughout its constituent sub-units, in relatively simple drill and formations.

From maniple to cohort

The cohort was a tactical grouping of three maniples: one of *hastati*, one of *principes* and one of *triarii*, the latter being brought up to a strength equal to that of the others. Cohorts of this type are first attested in the 3rd century BC, more than a hundred years before they became a permanent feature of the legion's organization (Polyb. 11.23.1). The Middle Republican cohort was an *ad hoc* grouping of not quite 500 men, a sort of 'miniature task force' to be employed in tactical situations that were unsuitable for a complete legion, but too demanding to be handled by a single maniple of perhaps 160 men. The later integration of the cohort into the formal organization of the Late Republican legion was a reflection of the many tactical situations in which the legion

The typical formation of the manipular legion, allowing maniples to advance and retreat through intervals in the battle lines. Note the smaller relative size of the maniples of *triarii* in the third line. (Author's drawing)

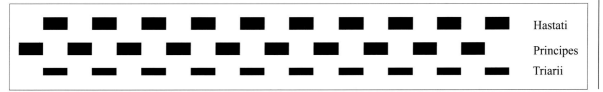

Hastati

Principes

Triarii

might find itself, ranging from full-scale field battles to circumstances that required the legion's manpower to be divided up and dispersed over quite a wide area, yet still in useful concentrations.

The permanent adoption of the cohort into the organization of the legion took place in the final decades of the 2nd century BC, and led to the division of the maniples into centuries: i.e., a withering away of the distinction between the three maniples forming a tactical cohort, and a new emphasis on the distinct identity of its six centuries. These centuries retained the old manipular designations of *hastatus*, *princeps* and *pilus* (another title for the *triarius*), and were further distinguished by the terms *prior* ('front') and *posterior* ('rear'); for instance, as late as c.AD 300 the epitaph of Aurelius Justinus of *legio XI Claudia* identifies his century as that of the *hastatus posterior* (*ILS* 2332). These titles suggest that pairs of centuries of the cohortal legion could form up one behind the other.

This may perhaps be confirmed by the formation of Arrian's army against the Alani in AD 135: four ranks of legionaries armed with heavy *pila* (*prior* centuries?) were backed by four ranks of legionaries (*posterior* centuries?) who threw light javelins over the heads of the leading ranks into the enemy cavalry beyond (Arr. *Acies Contra Alanos* 16–18).

Yet Arrian's array may not have been an arrangement of *prior* and *posterior* centuries. Caesar's report of the battle that he fought against the Belgae at the River Sabis in 57 BC could point to centuries fighting side by side. At one stage Caesar found that his hard-pressed troops had become bunched up and had no room to use their swords effectively. He accordingly gave the order '*Manipulos laxare*' – 'Open up the maniples!' (Caes. *BG* 2.25). This may have meant no more than 'open up the ranks'; but because of the circumstances of this battle – Caesar had been ambushed, and his army was formed into a loose single line – it seems probable that the centuries were drawn up side by side and, through a combination of enemy pressure and growing panic causing the troops to draw close to one another, the usual intervals necessary for unit cohesion had disappeared.

While not necessarily signifying fixed relative positions in the battle line, however, the terms *prior* and *posterior* do seem to indicate the close co-operation of two centuries in combat, one supporting the other.

The cohort's command structure

It has been suggested that the senior centurion of a cohort, the *pilus prior*, had command of the cohort (Goldsworthy 1996, 15–16); but there is no evidence whatsoever for this. The *pilus prior* may have had seniority, but this status was not a separate rank distinct from that of the other five centurions in the cohort. Because of ancient Rome's strictly classified system of social class, centurions could not command bodies of men larger than a century. The simple fact is that the legionary cohort of the Late Republic and Early Empire did not have a commander; and this is supported by the fact that neither did it have its own standard or *genius* ('spirit'). Each century had its own standard, which as well as being the essential focus of direction in battle was viewed as a divine totem embodying the *genius* of the century – just as the *genius* of the entire legion resided in the *aquila* (eagle standard). There are many instances of legionaries celebrating and worshipping the *genii* of the legion, and of their individual centuries; but there is no evidence at all for the *genius* of the cohort.

In his *Commentaries*, Caesar speaks of battle lines composed of cohorts or of groups of cohorts performing manoeuvres, and sometimes of single cohorts making charges. The cohort is therefore regularly described as the principal tactical unit of the Roman army; but how could it function as such without a commander? The cohort in action was much like the old manipular legion in action: its constituent units were trained to act in close co-operation, all of them probably responding to a fairly limited set of trumpet signals.

Grave *stele* of a *tesserarius* of *legio II Parthica*, 3rd century AD. Note that like the more senior *optio*, the centurion's second-in-command, this third officer of the century carries a long staff, possibly used in battle to shove soldiers back into line – like the halberds or half-pikes of NCOs in the 17th–19th centuries. (Steven D.P.Richardson)

Methods of defending the intervals within a cohort, with its centuries arranged in two possible variations of *prior* (front) and *posterior* (rear) order. The *posterior* centuries advance to cover the intervals, while the outside files of the *prior* centuries turn to face the attackers. (Author's drawing)

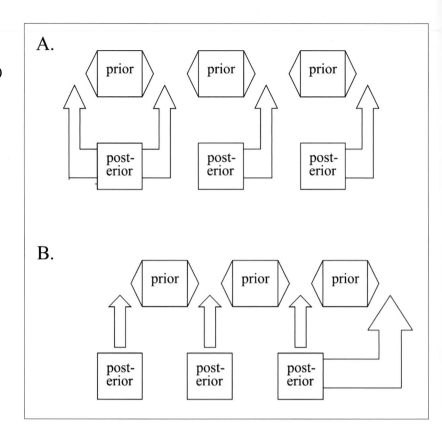

The cohortal legion did – eventually – have a permanent commander, called a *legatus*; but individual legionary cohorts never received commanders unless they were on detached operations. This seeming anomaly – the absence of 'middle management' from the legion – is logically explained by the limitations of communication on the battlefield. Once battle was joined the first battle line was often beyond the control of the general and his legates (cf Caes *BG* 1.52); the centurions each led as many soldiers as could be effectively commanded by a single man in the chaos of battle.

This contrasts with the infantry *cohortes* and cavalry *alae* of the auxiliary branch of the army; as they evolved during the 1st century AD, each of these was a distinct permanent unit within no permanent higher formation, and thus had its own commander, a *praefectus* or prefect (and therefore presumably its own standard). In modern terms, if we compare the legion to a division, then the auxiliary cohorts might be called 'corps assets' or 'divisional attachments', outside the formal divisional order of battle.

Basic battle formations

The Romans had a consistent and practical approach to the battle array of their armies. The formation employed against the African rebel Tacfarinas in AD 17 was typical (see Plates D/E): light infantry cohorts were arranged on either side of *legio III Augusta*, while cavalry formed the wings – hence *ala* ('wing') as the title of Imperial cavalry units (Tac. *Ann.* 2.52). This formation was used by the Pompeians in their final battle against Caesar at Munda in 45 BC, but on a much greater scale, as no fewer than 13 legions formed the centre (Anon. *BHisp.* 30). The formation was still current in the 3rd century AD, for example at the battle of Nisibis (Her. 4.15.1).

Sometimes the formation was simply cavalry on the flanks and heavy infantry in the centre, as at Mons Graupius (AD 84), where the fearsome Batavian and Tungrian auxiliary cohorts formed the centre of the line (Tac. *Agric.* 35). A variation on this basic theme was to mix light and heavy infantry in the centre; this was achieved by simply placing the light troops in the intervals that separated the sub-units of heavy infantry – as at the River Muthul in 109 BC (Sall. *BJ* 49.6), at Chaeronea in 86 BC (Front. *Strat.* 2.3.17) and also at Nisibis in AD 217 (see below, under 'Intervals in the battle line'). Light troops, or at least soldiers equipped with long-range missile weapons, could also be posted behind the heavy infantry in order to keep up a continuous 'fire' over the heads of the men in front – as in Arrian's array against the Alani in AD 135, or by both Roman armies at Issus in AD 194 (Arr. *Ectaxis* 17–18, 25; Dio 74.7.2–4; cf Plut. *Sulla* 18.4–6 for Chaeronea).

If one of the wings of an army was anchored on a natural or man-made obstacle, i.e. something that would prevent enemy outflanking manoeuvres, then cavalry would form only on the exposed flank of the infantry – as occurred at Pharsalus (48 BC), where Caesar's left and Pompey's right were secured by the steeply banked River Enipeus (Caes. *BC.* 3.86). At Uzitta (46 BC) the left wing of the Pompeian infantry extended to the walls of Uzitta town itself, requiring cavalry to be positioned only on their right; similarly, Caesar's opposing right was secured by fortified lines, and all of his cavalry was posted on the left opposite the Pompeian squadrons (Anon. *BAfr.* 59–60). On rare occasions Roman armies could be composed almost entirely of cavalry, and so both the centre and wings of a battle line would be formed by horsemen, as at Ruspina in 46 BC (Anon. *BAfr.* 13). Cavalry could also be used to form the centre in order to conceal the presence of infantry, as by Pompey the Great against the Albanians in 65 BC (Dio 37.4.2, see below).

Intervals in the battle line

Such intervals were necessary to maintain the cohesion of the units forming battle lines and to prevent them dissolving into a disorganized mass. It was easier for battle lines to advance and maintain formation if this was carried out by small mobile units acting in unison, rather than by a huge and unwieldy continuous line.

Intervals allowed light troops to make sallies against the enemy and then retreat to safety (Plut. *Ant.* 41.4–5). Intervals could also allow cavalry to pass through the ranks of the infantry and make frontal charges against the enemy (Front. *Strat.* 2.3.17; cf Livy 10.41 for this as the decisive tactic against the Samnites' elite Linen Legion at the battle of Aquilonia in 293 BC). At Nisibis (AD 217) the non-continuous battle line allowed the heavy infantry units (legions, praetorian and auxiliary cohorts) to maintain a strong defensive formation, while the light troops

Gravestone of Gnaeus Musius, *aquilifer* (eagle-bearer) of the Fourteenth Legion, *Gemina Martia Victrix*; in some inscriptions the number is rendered as *legio XIIII* instead of *XIV*. The *aquila* was the sacred embodiment of the *genius* or spirit of the legion, as the *signum* embodied the spirit of the century. Ancient sources frequently mention ritual honours being paid to these standards; the lack of any similar mention of legionary cohort standards is one reason to doubt that the latter was normally a recognized level of command. The eagle was sacred to jupiter, and Musius' shield is emblazoned with a winged thunderbolt, another symbol of the god. (RHC Archive)

postioned between them were free to make opportunist 'marauding sorties' against the Parthian archers and armoured cataphracts (see Plate G), some of whom were mounted on camels (Her. 4.15).

It might be wondered if an army maintaining gaps in its battle line did not run the risk of the enemy pouring through the gaps and surrounding individual sub-units. However, enemies who charged into an interval might find themselves caught in the 'crossfire' of missiles thrown by light troops (cf Livy 30.33.3); and – because legionaries were trained to fight as individuals, and to turn and meet attacks from all directions (Polyb. 18.32.10–11) – the files on either side of the penetration could simply turn inwards to face the danger and attack its flanks. Also, if the Roman army was drawn up in more than one battle line, the penetrating enemy would face an immediate counter-charge from the front. Of course, this all depended on the Romans holding their nerve and fighting back in an orderly fashion; if an enemy succeeded in establishing a penetration amongst the ranks, panic could quickly take hold. Even veteran legionaries found it disconcerting to be threatened on their unshielded (right-hand) side (Caes. *BC* 1.44).

Sometimes the enemy were actually lured into entering the intervals in the battle line, which would close up behind and trap them (e.g. at Chaeronea, App. *Mith.* 42). In 65 BC, Pompey exploited the gaps in his legionary lines to destroy the army of Oroeses, king of the Asiatic Albanians. Oroeses' army was not as big as Pompey's, but he did have more cavalry than the Roman general. Fearing that Oroeses would withdraw if he saw the full extent of the Roman army, Pompey advanced with only his cavalry and formed it into line. Oroeses made ready to attack the Roman squadrons before the infantry could be brought up; but unknown to him, the legions had already arrived, their progress being concealed by the cavalry lines, and with their helmets covered to prevent them glinting in the sun. The legionaries halted a little way behind their cavalry and knelt down in close order.

When Oroeses' cavalry charged the Roman troopers retreated before them; exultant at their easy victory, the Albanians thundered on in confident pursuit. But the legionaries had now risen from their concealed position and formed a battle line with intervals; the *turmae* (cavalry squadrons of 30 riders) at the centre of the Roman cavalry line passed through the intervals – and so did a considerable number of pursuing Albanians, who were duly surrounded. The rest of Oroeses' cavalry drew rein before the Roman infantry, but before they could re-form they were attacked from behind by those Roman *turmae* that had formed the left and right wings of Pompey's original cavalry line. These troopers had not gone through their infantry formation but had ridden down its flanks; they now wheeled about, and hit Oroeses' bewildered horsemen as they milled in confusion (Dio 37.4; Front. *Strat.* 2.3.14).

The epitaph of Aurelius Justinius of legio XI Claudia, c.AD 300. Even at this late date the inscription refers (lines 4 to 5) to his cohort and century – that of the *hastatus posterior*. (Stephen D.P.Richardson)

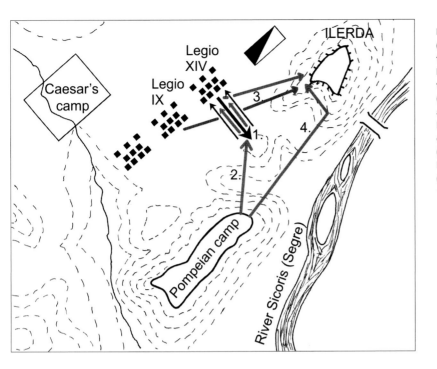

The size of intervals

When the old manipular legion formed up for battle, the maniples were
separated by intervals probably equalling the frontage of a maniple –
if a maniple of 120 men formed six ranks, then c.60ft in close order,
and 120ft in open order – the gap being covered by the maniple in the
following line (Polyb. 15.9.7–9). The result was a *quincunx* or chessboard
formation. Intervals were maintained between legionary cohorts (cf Caes.
BG 5.15, where the implication of the passage is that the interval was
much smaller than usual); and there must also have been intervals
between the centuries, to maintain their individual cohesion. The
manipular legion had a system for replacing exhausted battle lines:

> When the battle formation of the army was completed, the *hastati*
> were the first to engage. If they failed to repulse the enemy, they
> slowly retired through the intervals between the maniples of the
> *principes* who then took up the fight, the *hastati* following in their
> rear. The *triarii*, meantime, were resting on one knee under their
> standards, their shields over their shoulders and their spears
> planted on the ground with the points upwards, giving them
> the appearance of a bristling palisade. If the *principes* were also
> unsuccessful, they slowly retired to the *triarii*, which has given rise
> to the proverbial saying, when people are in great difficulty, that
> 'matters have come down to the *triarii*'. When the *triarii* had
> admitted the *hastati* and *principes* through the intervals separating
> their maniples, they rose from their kneeling posture and,
> instantly closing their maniples up, they blocked all passage
> through them, and in one compact mass fell on the enemy as
> the last hope of the army. The enemy who had followed up the
> others, as though they had defeated them, saw with dread a new
> and larger army rising apparently out of the earth (Livy 8.8.9–13).

Scene from Trajan's Column, which was decorated with a spiral frieze charting the course of the Dacian Wars, AD 101–102 and 105–106. Here legionary reserves are led into action by standard-bearers (top right), while a wounded legionary and auxiliary are treated by medical orderlies (bottom centre right). (RHC Archive)

The replacement of whole or segments of battle lines made up of cohorts is reported by Caesar, whose legions regularly formed up in three lines – a 4-3-3 formation of cohorts. It seems unlikely that cohorts were separated by intervals the same size as the frontage of a cohort. Line replacement of the type that occurred at Pharsalus – where Caesar's third line of cohorts moved to the front and relieved the first and second lines (Caes. *BC* 3.94) – seems more feasible if the centuries were separated by intervals equalling their frontage (or a little bigger), so that they could move back or forward in the manner described by Livy for maniples. If cohorts did deploy with century-sized gaps between the centuries (and perhaps therefore only the same between adjacent cohorts), then the appearance of a cohortal legion (see Plates D/E) would not have been very different from that of a manipular legion.

Livy's description of the tactics of the manipular legions ends with the maniples closing up into a single, unbroken line. The legions may have done this at the final stage of the battle of Zama (202 BC), delivering one last massed charge of irresistible weight (Livy 30.34.11–13). Cohorts, and the centuries that made them up, could also form unbroken lines, for example in Arrian's closed defensive formation against the Alani. At Ilerda (49 BC) three cohorts of the

Ninth Legion were forced to fight shoulder-to-shoulder on the narrow uphill approach to the town. Despite these close confines, Caesar still managed to replace exhausted cohorts with fresh (this battle against the Pompeians lasted for five hours). Unfortunately Caesar does not tell us how the withdrawal and replacement of cohorts was done; perhaps it was achieved by removing one century at a time? This battle was mostly fought with missiles, and the duration of the fighting suggests that there must have been some lulls, allowing replacements to come up in relative safety (Caes. *BC* 1.45–46).

LEGIONARY BATTLE LINES AND MANOEUVRES

Simplex acies

The Romans called their battle lines *acies* – in Latin this apt term means the sharp edge of a sword. The most basic was the *simplex acies*, the 'simple' or single line of cohorts. During the Late Republic this was often a battle line of necessity, used when an army was too small to deploy into two or more lines, or when faced with a larger and more mobile opponent – for example, Caesar's army at Ruspina in 46 BC (see below). Sometimes a large army might have to fight in a *simplex acies*, in order to deploy rapidly and meet a surprise attack, such as that which confronted Caesar when the Belgae ambushed his legions at the River Sabis (57 BC).

The *simplex acies* was sometimes forced on commanders by undisciplined soldiers, as happened at the battle of **Forum Gallorum** (43 BC). On spotting the Second and Thirty-Fifth Legions of Mark Antony concealed in marshy woodland on either side of the Via Aemilia, the *legio Martia* and two praetorian cohorts deployed from their marching column into a single line of 12 cohorts. Enraged at the

Battle of Forum Gallorum, 43 BC. The *legio Martia* and Hirtius' praetorian cohort held Antony's two complete legions at bay, but Octavian's praetorian cohort was destroyed. (Author's drawing)

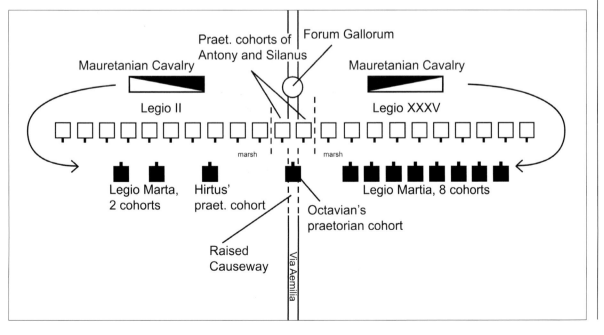

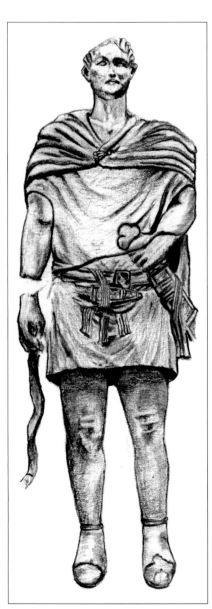

attempt to ambush them, these units ignored orders to hold back, and advanced on the enemy. The nature of the terrain meant that eight cohorts of the *legio Martia* formed the right wing of the battle line on the marshy ground to the right of the road; the praetorian cohort of Octavian (adopted son and heir of Julius Caesar) formed the centre, on the raised causeway of the Via Aemilia; and the left, also in marshy ground on the other side of the road, was formed by the two remaining cohorts of the *legio Martia* and the praetorian cohort of the consul Hirtius. This battle line suggests that the eight cohorts of the *legio Martia* had formed the head of the marching column, the praetorian cohorts following, and the other two legionary cohorts bringing up the rear. These units were acting as the escort to four newly raised legions, and the veterans of the *legio Martia* ('legion of Mars') bluntly told the recruits to keep out of the way.

Facing the eight cohorts of the *legio Martia* was Antony's complete *legio XXXV*, but despite its extra two cohorts the Antonian legion was forced back. Appian's grim description of the hand-to-hand combat is famous:

They met together in close order, and since neither could dislodge the other, they locked together with their swords as if in a wrestling contest. If a man fell, he was immediately carried away and another took his place. The legionaries had no need of encouragement or cheering on, for each man's experience made him his own general. When they tired, they separated for a few moments to recover as if they were engaged in training exercises, and then grappled with each other again (Appian, *Civil Wars* 3.68).

However, the 'Martians' (as they were called) found themselves 500 paces from their original position, having advanced so far that Antony's Mauretanian cavalry threatened to outflank them and attack them in the rear. Now the legionaries finally listened to orders and started to fall back, apparently by stepping back a few paces at a time. The Antonian legionaries were evidently so exhausted that they did not give immediate pursuit, and the Martians were able to turn about while light troops – i.e. unarmoured soldiers armed with slings, bows or light javelins – held the Mauretanian cavalry back with a shower of missiles. Although our sources do not make it clear, these light troops were presumably auxiliaries attached to the *legio Martia*; however, some 300–400 men per legion were sometimes lightly equipped (*expediti*) for use in a variety of skirmishing and anti-cavalry roles (e.g. Caes. *BC* 3.75, 84 and Anon. *BAfr.* 75).

The fighting on the left followed a similar course, with the two cohorts of the *legio Martia* and Hirtius' praetorian cohort at first holding their own against the complete veteran *legio II*, before making a successful withdrawal. However, Octavian's praetorian cohort on the Via Aemilia in the centre found itself pitted against two other praetorian cohorts, those of Antony and his ally Junius Silanus, and was destroyed (Cic. *Fam.* 10.30; App. *BC* 3.67–69).

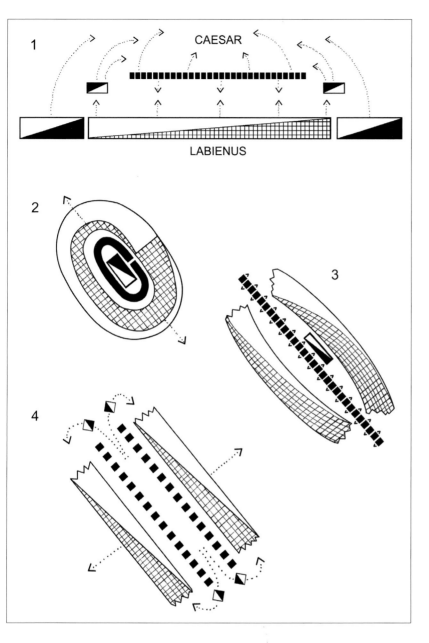

Battle of Ruspina, 46 BC.
(1) Labienus' predominantly mounted force surrounds Caesar's *simplex acies*.
(2) Caesar's force contracts into an oval *orbis* – though the author doubts that it was actually this shape.
(3) Every second Caesarian cohort turns about.
(4) The *simplex acies* is transformed into a *duplex acies*, and the Caesarians break out of the encirclement. (Author's drawing after Veith, 1906)

Julius Caesar's favourite battle array was the *triplex acies* (see below), but at **Ruspina (46 BC)** the small size of his expeditionary army compelled him to form a *simplex acies* when confronted by a far greater force of Pompeian cavalry and light infantry under Labienus. The ensuing battle was desperate, yet it illustrates how effective legionary cohorts arrayed in *simplex acies* could be – when directed by a master tactician.

The Pompeians advanced in a single line of extraordinary length, seemingly with infantry in the centre and a considerable force of cavalry on either flank. As the line neared the Caesarians it became apparent that the centre of the Pompeian army was actually composed of cavalry in exceptionally close order interspersed with light infantry – Numidian javelineers. To avoid being enveloped at the first onset, Caesar formed his three legions into a *simplex acies* of 30 cohorts. His 150 archers – rapidly summoned from the fortified camp at Ruspina when the dust cloud thrown up by the Pompeians was first spotted – formed a thin screen before the line of cohorts. Caesar had only 400 cavalry; these were divided between the flanks, tasked with preventing the overwhelming cavalry of the enemy from outflanking the battle line. Eventually, that is what happened; the Caesarian troopers fought desperately and extended their line until it became too thin to hold the Pompeians back, and the enemy's *corona* ('crown' – an encircling manoeuvre) was successful.

While the cavalry fought in vain to prevent envelopment, Caesar's cohorts received the combined frontal charge of the Pompeian cavalry and Numidian light troops. The cavalry attacked, disengaged, then wheeled about and attacked again; the Numidians held the ground they gained and bombarded the legionaries with javelins. The Caesarian infantry counter-attacked; but their sallies and futile pursuit of cavalrymen disordered the battle line, and Caesar passed orders that no man was to advance more than four paces from the standards. (Presumably the archers had been received into the ranks of the legionaries before the enemy charge.)

Once surrounded, the Caesarians huddled together, the centuries closing up perhaps in *orbis* formation (see below). Titus Labienus had been Caesar's ablest lieutenant during the conquest of Gaul, but was his bitterest enemy in the subsequent civil war; now he rode up to the front rank of Caesar's troops. It seems that all three of these legions were

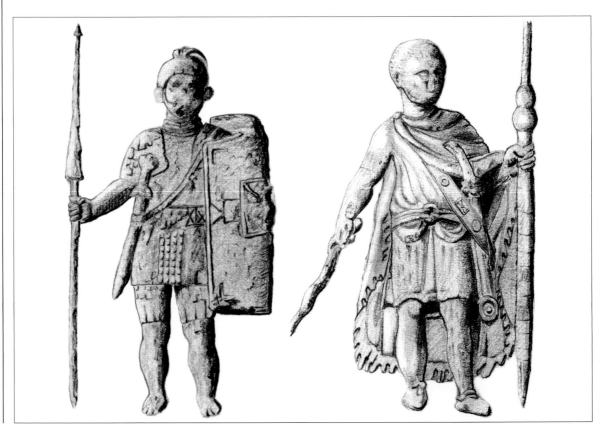

formed of recent recruits, and Labienus was taunting the frightened young men; but he was confronted by a veteran who had formerly served in the Tenth Legion – Caesar's favourite. Killing Labienus' horse with his *pilum*, this seasoned legionary shouted 'That'll teach you, Labienus, that it's a soldier of the Tenth that you're dealing with!' This detail of the battle is noteworthy in that it suggests that new legions were being formed around a cadre of veterans. Also, despite there being no clear evidence for file leaders of the type common in Hellenistic and Late Roman armies, it suggests that the front rank in Late Republican and Early Imperial armies was composed of experienced veterans (cf. Pistoria, below).

Caesar was now surrounded by a larger and more mobile force – in an echo of Rome's terrible defeat by Hannibal's Carthaginians at Cannae (216 BC) – and some of his green recruits were beginning to falter; but before the enemy closed in, Caesar gave the order to extend the battle line as far as possible. Extending line was achieved by reducing the depth of the files and bringing men forward between them. A late Roman tactical manual stated that extending the line of an army in close order was a time-consuming manoeuvre (*Strategicon* 12.B.17), but on this occasion the young soldiers seem to have accomplished it quickly. Caesar then ordered every second cohort to turn about, so that its standards were to the rear. Having about-turned, the rear rank of each cohort now faced the enemy, and presumably the *optiones* assumed leadership of their centuries. Caesar had effectively transformed his single line of cohorts into a *duplex acies* or double battleline (one is irresistibly reminded of the British 28th Foot at Alexandria in 1801, when the Glosters won their unique 'back badge').

Meanwhile, his cavalry appear to have broken through the encirclement, and the Pompeians were forced to form into two lines to counter the new cohort formation. The divided Pompeians were then scattered by a sudden charge and hail of missiles from each of Caesar's battle lines. The legionaries and cavalry gave pursuit over a short distance, but not so far as to become disordered and vulnerable to counter-attack; then Caesar started to fall back to his fortified camp at Ruspina, three miles distant.

The Pompeians rallied when Marcus Petreius and Gnaeus Piso appeared with reinforcements of 1,600 cavalry and a large number of infantry, and moved to harry the rear of the Caesarians. Caesar's army was retreating in battle formation, but it is not clear if it was still in two lines; when the Pompeians came up, Caesar ordered his army to turn about and renew the battle. As before, the Caesarians were encircled, but the Pompeians refused to come to close quarters, preferring to wear

A soldier equipped with a flat oval shield and light javelins. Conventionally interpreted as showing an auxiliary, this carving – one of a series on column bases from the late 1st century AD legionary headquarters building at Mainz – may in fact depict a light-armed legionary; such *expediti* are mentioned in Julius Caesar's army. (Photo Jasper Oorthuys)

Gravestone of Q.Luccius Faustus, a *signifer* (standard-bearer) of the Fourteenth Legion from Upper Germany, where the *legio Gemina Martia Victrix* was based before AD 43. Note the caped doubling at the shoulders of his mail shirt; the face-mask on his helmet, which is also covered with the skin of an animal head, its paws falling over his shoulders; his small oval shield; and his sword – see page 62, left hand example. The inscription tells us that he died at the age of 35, after 17 years of service. This monument has often been studied as evidence for the appearance of centurial standards. The six discs, set between the wreathed motif at the top and the Capricorn decoration and apparent tassels at the bottom, suggest a temptingly simple interpretation – that the number of discs indicated the number of the century within the cohort; but ancient sources do not confirm this, and other explanations are possible. (RHC Archive)

down their opponents with missiles; Caesar's men may have formed *testudo* to counter this (the 'tortoise' formation, where the inner ranks lifted their shields over their heads and overlapped them to form a protective roof – see below). As the Pompeians' supply of missiles diminished and their energy for the fight waned, Caesar encouraged his men to prepare for another break-out; he readied the surviving cavalry and some select cohorts to attack on a given signal, and this time ordered them to keep up their pursuit (Anon. *BAfr*. 11–18). It is not clear if this was a massed attack at a single point of the Pompeian circle, or a simultaneous attack at many points, but the result was decisive:

> In a moment they drove the enemy off the plain without difficulty, and forced them beyond the high ground, and won the position [i.e. the high ground]. After remaining there for a short time, they retired slowly in battle formation to their own entrenchments (Anon., *The African War* 18).

* * *

An example of a foolish failure to employ the *simplex acies* was the battle of **Carrhae (53 BC)**, when Gaius Cassius Longinus counselled Marcus Licinius Crassus to deploy his army in that formation to engage the Parthians' horse archers and cataphracts. (Infamous to history as a leader in the assassination of Caesar, Cassius proved his military ability by retrieving the situation on the Parthian front after Carrhae.) 'Extend the legionaries as far as possible across the plain in a shallow line', he advised Crassus, 'and put the cavalry on either flank; that will prevent the enemy from surrounding us'. Initially Crassus followed this advice – but then changed his mind, and rearranged the seven legions into a hollow square formation (perhaps known as the *orbis* – see below). Each legion had eight cohorts present, since two were detached on garrison duties elsewhere; each side of the huge square was formed of 12 cohorts, and another eight were stationed outside its left flank, along with 500 light troops, and 1,300 of the best cavalry, to act as a mobile force. There were probably about 4,000 cavalry and 4,000 archers, slingers and javelinmen in total, and cavalry and light troops were attached to each cohort in the formation, probably positioned in the intervals between them.

Readers familiar with the outcome of the battle may be surprised to learn that at Carrhae the Romans outnumbered the Parthians by three to one. The Parthian general, the Surena, had 1,000 armoured cataphracts and 10,000 horse archers – but also a train of 1,000 camels laden with arrows to replenish their quivers. On the Mesopotamian plains cavalry were free to hit and run, and Crassus' decision to form square was foolish in the extreme. The Parthian cataphracts readily swatted his light troops aside, then withdrew as their horse archers came up and began to bring the Roman formation under a withering arrow-storm, gradually moving to envelop it.

Strangely, although the Romans formed a close shield wall (with each man occupying half the usual space so that the rim of his shield was hard against that of his neighbour), it does not seem that they formed *testudo*, for many were wounded by arrows shot at a steep angle to drop down on to them. Crassus' legionaries, unaware of the camel train, expected the archers to exhaust their supply of shafts soon, and presumably wanted to be able to deploy rapidly for the counter-attack. (Yet Mark Antony used the hollow square in *testudo* to great effect against the Parthian archery in 36 BC, and his veteran legionaries were able to charge out from their 'tortoise' rapidly – experience was perhaps the key to this contradiction, since Crassus' legions were probably new formations.)

As their true dilemma became clearer, Crassus ordered his son Publius to take the force of cavalry and cohorts stationed outside the square to charge the enemy. The Parthian cavalry fell back before the attack, raising dust and drawing Publius' cavalry into a trap; they far outstripped the legionary cohorts, and blindly ran into the volleys of the horse archers, who had halted their apparent flight. The Roman troopers pressed on, but were then met by the cataphracts and at length were put to flight; turning back the way they had come, they reunited with the detached cohorts of legionaries and retreated to a small hill. The legionaries and dismounted troopers formed a shield wall around it but, because the slopes were steep and bumpy, and the horses were in the centre, it was neither a strong wall nor a roofed *testudo*, and was gradually destroyed by the Parthian archers. Publius, wounded and despairing, ordered his shield-bearer (i.e. the servant who followed him in battle with a remount and spare weapons) to kill him so that he would not fall into the hands of the enemy alive.

When the Parthians overran the hill Publius' head was cut off, stuck on the point of a cataphract's lance, and carried around the main Roman formation to torment Crassus. With the best cavalry destroyed, and the sallies of the remaining horsemen and light troops from its ranks half-hearted and ineffective, Crassus' square was now tormented on all sides by the horse archers until nightfall. Despite this sustained mauling, the Roman square was not broken – perhaps it had finally formed into a *testudo*. Under the cover of darkness the decision was made to abandon the 4,000 wounded and leave the dead unburied; this was shameful in the extreme, as it violated the Roman military oath, and was indicative of a total collapse of morale.

The survivors retreated safely to the city of Carrhae, but were forced to abandon it the following evening due to lack of supplies, and retreated towards the Armenian foothills. It was during this second confused and panicky night retreat that the Roman army fell apart, and

Gravestone of Aurelius Alexys, a heavy infantryman of an elite cohort of Spartans, who may have been killed at Nisibis in AD 217. (Author's photo)

the following day the Parthians picked off the isolated groups of cohorts. Crassus was briefly saved from capture when a senior officer named Octavius, who had succeeded in leading 5,000 legionaries to a strong hill position, left his strongpoint to aid Crassus' hard-pressed band of fugitives on the level ground; he drove off the Parthians, and surrounded the general with a proper *testudo*, boasting that 'No Parthian arrow can strike our general now!'

The Parthians became dispirited at their inability to break the formation as it slowly drew nearer to the safety of broken, hilly terrain unsuitable for their tactics. The Surena called off the attacks, coming in person – with his bow symbolically unstrung – to offer negotiations for a Roman withdrawal. Plutarch tells us that Crassus was suspicious of this offer, believing that the Parthians would anyway have to stop fighting when the approaching night fell, but his exhausted troops nevertheless demanded that he agree to the parly. Crassus went forward warily, accompanied by Octavius and a few other officers; but the offer was indeed a trap. Plutarch states that a Parthian called Promaxathres struck Crassus down, but the historian Dio quoted a suggestion that he was actually killed by his own men in order to prevent the disgrace of a Roman general falling into the hands of the enemy.

Those troops who had urged Crassus to treat with the Surena either surrendered themselves, or scattered under cover of darkness. Only a few made it back to Roman territory (including Cassius, with a handful of cavalry); from a field army of more than 30,000 soldiers, some 20,000 were killed and 10,000 passed into slavery (Plut. *Crass.* 23–31; Dio 40.21–27).

At **Nisibis (AD 217)** – the last battle the Romans ever fought against the Parthians before the latter were overthrown by the Sassanian Persians – the Roman army formed exactly as Cassius had advocated before Carrhae. For three days it resisted every attempt by the Parthian cavalry to envelop its flanks, by continually extending line and manoeuvring a strong force of cavalry to protect each wing (Her. 4.15.1–5). Nisibis ended in stalemate, with the opposing armies exhausted and the battlefield so littered with the bodies of men, horses and camels that it was impossible to advance across it.

V	IV	III	II	I
X	IX	VIII	VII	VI

Duplex acies

As well as Caesar's novel use of the *duplex acies* at Ruspina, it was also employed against him by a Pompeian general during the final stage of the **Ilerda campaign (49 BC)** in Spain. Lucius Afranius confronted Caesar with five legions in *duplex acies*, each legion presumably in a 5-5 formation of cohorts – 25 cohorts in each of the two battle lines. Afranius also had a third reserve line of Spanish auxiliary cohorts, but this was presumably some distance behind the legionary formation; Caesar clearly did not consider Afranius' army as being drawn up in a triple battle line. If the third line of auxiliaries was a reserve – and presumably a static one, whereas the legionary formation was to be mobile – then the second line of legionary cohorts must have been intended to support, reinforce and, if necessary, to relieve/replace the first line. The second line could also turn about or wheel to face an enemy coming at the rear or flanks, and so fight as a *simplex acies.*

The late 4th or early 5th century AD writer Vegetius applies the *duplex acies* 5-5 formation of cohorts to his description of the *legio antiqua* – 'the ancient legion'. It has been suggested that this element of his problematical description was derived from an early Imperial source and therefore represents the typical battle array of the Imperial legions. In Vegetius' *duplex acies*, the more powerful first cohort is positioned on the right of the first line. The fifth cohort holds the left, and accordingly has stronger soldiers than cohorts two, three and four. The sixth and tenth cohorts hold the right and left of the second line respectively, and also contain the strongest soldiers because of the potential vulnerability of the flanks (Veg. *Epit.* 2.6, 18).

However, the *duplex acies* does not receive ready confirmation in the battle accounts of the first three centuries AD. In fact, we are generally much more poorly served by the surviving Imperial sources for battle arrays. Tacitus' account of Mons Graupius (AD 84) seems fairly clear: a *simplex acies* of auxiliary cohorts, and the legions held back in reserve (Tac. *Agric* 35). From Tacitus' accounts of the two battles of Cremona during the civil war of AD 69 we are again left with the impression of the opposing armies in *simplex acies*, though the use of reserves is mentioned at the first battle (*Hist.* 2.43).

Tacitus goes into some detail about the marching order of Germanicus' army as it proceeded to the battle of Idistaviso (AD 16). The marching column (*agmen*) was arranged so that the legions, praetorian cohorts and auxiliary units could simply turn or wheel into battle line; however, the brief description of the battle itself does not suggest anything other than a *simplex acies*. Admittedly, the descriptions of all the above battles are essentially so vague about cohort deployment that, for all we can tell, the cohorts of Germanicus'

Julius Caesar: a masterful tactician, he outfought all his opponents through skilful use of legions drawn up in *simplex*, *duplex*, and even *quadruplex acies*. (RHC Archive)

(A) Battle of Mons Graupius, AD 84. Auxiliary cohorts and *alae* in a *simplex acies*, with the legions in reserve.

(B) Arrian's formation against the Alani, AD 135.
(1, 2) Flank guards, auxiliary cohorts and archers on hills each side of main body.
(3) Catapults.
(A) Arrian and his bodyguards.
(Author's drawing, after Maxwell, 1990)

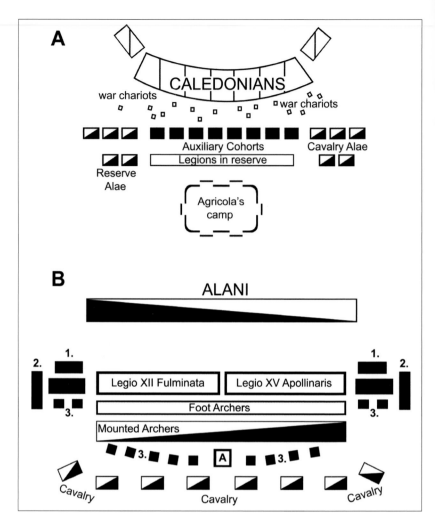

legions might have been arranged in more than one line (*Ann.* 2.16–17; cf 13.40 for Corbulo's marching-cum-battle formation in Armenia).

When the soldier-emperor Maximinus marched into rebellious Italy in AD 238, he advanced on the city of Emona in an *agmen quadratum*. This was a hollow square or rectangular marching formation, with the baggage protected in the centre; but such marching formations were also designed to deploy readily into battle lines. Maximinus' formation was a shallow rectangle: legionary infantry formed the front; Maximinus was at the rear with the praetorians and other guard units; and the sides were formed by cavalry and light troops, including cataphracts and horse archers. Maximinus' *agmen quadratum*, like all such formations, was therefore effectively a *duplex acies* (Her. 8.1.1–2) with cavalry wings; however, it clearly was not a *duplex acies* based on 5-5 arrangements of legionary cohorts.

* * *

In Arrian's description of the battle line that he drew up against the migrating **Alani (AD 135)**, he tells us that the legionaries were formed in eight tight ranks. However, the legionaries had marched to the battlefield four abreast, and when in battle formation the leading four ranks were armed with *pila* while the rear four ranks had *lanceae* or light javelins (Arr. *Acies* 5–6, 15–18). Perhaps we have here the normal components of a legionary *duplex acies*, but closed up immediately one behind the other so as to form a strong single line?

If so, Arrian's unusually close array suggests that the Imperial centuries of 80 men were formed in four ranks and 20 files. It may be that the leading ranks in Arrian's formation were the *prior* (front) centuries, and the rear ranks formed by the aptly titled *posterior* centuries (i.e. each pair of centuries forming a maniple). However, another possibility is that the centuries of each cohort were formed up side by side, so those in the leading ranks (from right to left) were of cohorts one to five, and those in the following ranks were of cohorts six to ten. There is, indeed, yet another possibility. The eight ranks could point to the files being formed by *contubernia*, the tent groups of eight men, ten of which comprised a century. This would mean that each century deployed in eight ranks and ten files, and also indicates that there could be a differentiation of armament within a century.

Triplex and quadruplex acies

In his account of the face-off with Afranius' legionary *duplex acies* at **Ilerda (49 BC)** – the two armies did not in the end come to blows – Caesar describes how his legionary cohorts were drawn up in a proper *triplex acies*: 'Caesar's line was triple; but four cohorts from each of the five legions

Typical patterns used in the reconstruction of the 4-3-3 cohort *triplex acies* formation for a legion. One suspects that intervals equalling the frontage of a cohort would be dangerously large in battle. (Author's drawing)

formed the first line, followed by three from each, and three more again' (*BC* 1.83). This 4-3-3 arrangement of cohorts has been taken to be the standard for a legion in *triplex acies* formation. It obviously developed from the triple-line formation of the manipular legion, which was used in the field – perhaps for the last time – at the battle of the **River Muthul (109 BC)**, where Caecilus Metellus (father of the Metellus who fought Sertorius in 76–75 BC – see below) fought against the rebel Numidian prince Jugurtha. However, in the final stage of that battle the extended manipular array was unsuitable for driving Jugurtha's infantry from its position on a hill, and Metellus grouped the maniples into cohorts. The charge of four cohorts was sufficient to dislodge the Numidians from the high ground (Sall. *Jug.* 49–52).

Cornelius Sulla is reputed to have employed a triple line against the Pontic phalanx and chariots at the battle of **Chaeronea (86 BC)** (Front. *Strat.* 2.3.17, also mixing in details from the subsequent battle at Orchomenus). Frontinus – himself a general in the mid 1st century AD – writes that Sulla's first line was made up of *antesignani* ('those who fight before the standards'), which was another term for the *hastati* (cf Livy 10.27.9).

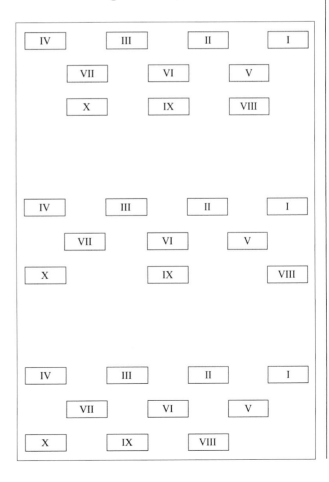

23

Battle scene from Trajan's Column, early 2nd century AD, showing mail-shirted Roman auxiliaries with oval shields, fighting with swords and (top left) bows; at left is a half-naked allied or auxiliary tribesman using a simple club. Note the wounded Dacian warriors being carried out of the fight (right). Jupiter (top centre) intervenes on behalf of the Romans to throw a thunderbolt at the enemy. (RHC Archive)

The second line was formed by *postsignani* ('those who fight behind the standards'). Was Sulla's battle line, then, essentially manipular? However, another source reports that he posted reserve legionary cohorts behind the cavalry on the wings to counter flank attacks (Plut. *Sulla* 17.7). Also, the term *antesignani* was still employed in Caesar's day and long into the Imperial period, when it probably meant no more than soldiers who fought in the front rank (e.g. Caes. *BC* 1.43); so Frontinus' terms may simply refer to the first and second lines of cohorts.

A *triplex acies* of the type described by Caesar may have been formed by the legions of the rebel Sergius Catilina when he was cornered by the consular army led by Marcus Petreius at **Pistoria (62 BC)**. Catilina had two legions and he formed a main battle line of eight cohorts, presumably four cohorts from each legion. Were the rest of the cohorts drawn up in groups of three? It is possible, but all we know is that the remaining cohorts were held in reserve in close order. Catilina's legions were under strength and only a quarter of his men were fully armed; the number of cohorts in his main battle line may not have been determined by a 4-3-3 *triplex acies* arrangement, but by the number of better equipped legionaries available to him, and perhaps also by the terrain in which the battle was fought. Outnumbered and lacking cavalry, Catilina formed up in a defile with steep, broken ground on either side so that he could not be outflanked.

Interestingly, Catilina's front rank was formed by veteran centurions and *evocati* – the latter were veterans who were specially recalled to service by their old commander (Catilina had been one of Sulla's senior officers). So as at Ruspina, at Pistoria we find the most experienced soldiers in the front rank – men who could be relied upon to hold their ground, to lead charges and to guide manoeuvres (Sall. *Cat.* 59.1–3).

It is only with Caesar's accounts of his conquest of Gaul and his civil war against the Senate and the Pompeians that we are presented with clear descriptions of Late Republican armies in battle array; but the *triplex acies* of cohorts was instrumental in some of Caesar's greatest victories.

Caesar's first major battle in the Gallic War serves to illustrate the usefulness of the *triplex acies*. When fighting the Helvetii and their allies near **Bibracte (58 BC)**, Caesar formed his army up on a hill. Four veteran legions (the Seventh, Eighth, Ninth and Tenth) were arrayed in a *triplex acies* halfway down the slope; the two new legions of recruits (the Eleventh and Twelfth) and all the auxiliaries were posted behind an earth rampart at the summit. The Helvetian host, perhaps c.77,000 strong if Caesar's figures are to be believed, advanced on the Roman position in what Caesar describes as a phalanx. The warriors were so tightly packed that their shields overlapped, and when they came into range of the Romans' *pila* some of the heavy javelins drove through two overlapped shields at a time, pinning them together and rendering them useless. The *pila* volley shattered the cohesion of the leading Helvetian ranks, and the Romans immediately drew their swords and charged down the slope at the run. Shieldless and mostly unarmoured, the Helvetii were eventually forced to retreat, themselves making for a hill a mile distant.

The legionaries were following, confident of victory, when they were struck in their exposed right flank by 15,000 Tulingi and Boii warriors who had formed a reserve. These slammed into the exposed Roman right (i.e. the unshielded side), and moved on the rear or third line of cohorts. The Helvetii, seeing this beneficial turn of events from their new hill position, raced back to tackle their erstwhile pursuers and close

Caesar's battle against the Helvetii, 58 BC. The third line of cohorts in the *triplex acies* wheels to engage the Tulingi and Boii. (Author's drawing, after G.Long, *Caesar's Commentaries, Books I–III*, 1857)

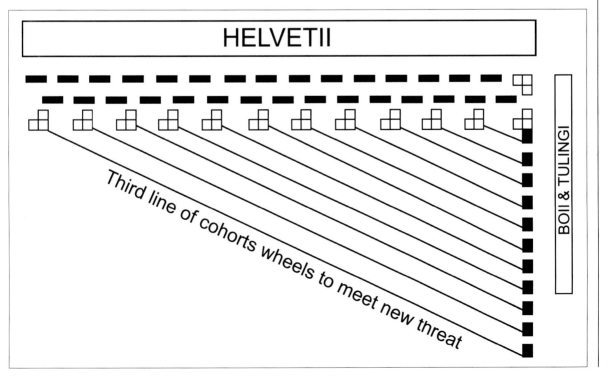

HELVETII

BOII & TULINGI

Third line of cohorts wheels to meet new threat

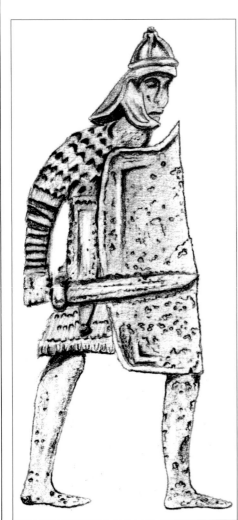

the pincer movement. Perhaps at the command of Caesar himself or one of his senior officers, or at the direction of their centurions drawing upon long experience (cf Caes. *BG* 2.21), the veterans in the third line of cohorts then wheeled to face the Tulingi and Boii, while the first and second lines pressed on to resume the fight with the revitalized Helvetii. Two battles were fought simultaneously, one on the right by *simplex acies*, the other at the front by *duplex acies*; in both the Romans were eventually successful, the enemy being slaughtered and their camp ransacked (Caes. *BG* 1.24–26).

Later in 58 BC Caesar deployed all six legions in a *triplex acies*, when fighting the German king **Ariovistus** (Caes. *BG* 1.51–53). Like the Helvetii, Ariovistus' Germans formed a dense, close-order phalanx; but because Caesar had offered battle so near to the German camp, and because the onset of the enemy was so swift, the legionaries had no time to open combat with their customary volley of *pila*. The javelins were dropped, swords drawn and a counter-charge launched. Both armies were victorious on their right, traditionally the stronger wing in ancient armies. The hard-pressed Roman left was rescued by the quick thinking of P.Licinius Crassus (later killed at Carrhae – see above):

> Young Publius Crassus, who was in command of the cavalry, noticed this, and because he could move more easily than the officers who were engaged between the battle lines, he sent the third line to aid our struggling men. So the battle was restored and all of the enemy turned and fled, not ceasing in their flight until they reached the River Rhine, some five miles away (Caesar, *Gallic War* 1.52–53).

As before, the intervention of the third line of cohorts had saved the day, but in this battle it not clear exactly what the third line did. Perhaps they moved forward and somehow relieved the embattled cohorts of the first and second lines, which may have been compressed into a single line because of the pressure of the Germans. Or perhaps the third line marched out to the left, wheeled, and attacked the flank of the Germans.

Caesar sometimes marched his army in a triple column, not only because it was easier and quicker to march with a broad front rather than in a single long column, but because such an *agmen* could wheel directly into a *triplex acies* (Caes. *BG* 4.14; cf Polyb 6.40.1–14).

* * *

At the monumental battle of **Pharsalus (48 BC)**, where Caesar faced Pompey and the forces of the Senate, both generals arranged their armies in *triplex acies*, but it was Caesar who exploited the potential of the formation to win a crushing victory over a larger foe. As mentioned above, Caesar's eight legions were greatly reduced in strength, numbering on average only 2,750 men each; and *legio IX* and *legio VIII* were so depleted from the hard fighting at

Dyrrhachium that they were positioned very close together in the line 'as if to make a single legion out of the two, and each was instructed to protect the other'. Pompey had 11 legions, each with a strength of about 4,000; but contrary to the usual offensive Roman tactics, he planned to use them as a static wall on which to pin the Caesarian infantry. Each line was ten ranks deep; this is the only instance where the depth of a Late Republican battle line is revealed, but because of the defensive tactics it may have been deeper than usual.

Pompey put his faith in his 7,000 cavalry. Massed on the left of his line (the right was secured by the River Enipeus), and backed by the 'firepower' of a large force of archers and slingers, the cavalry would

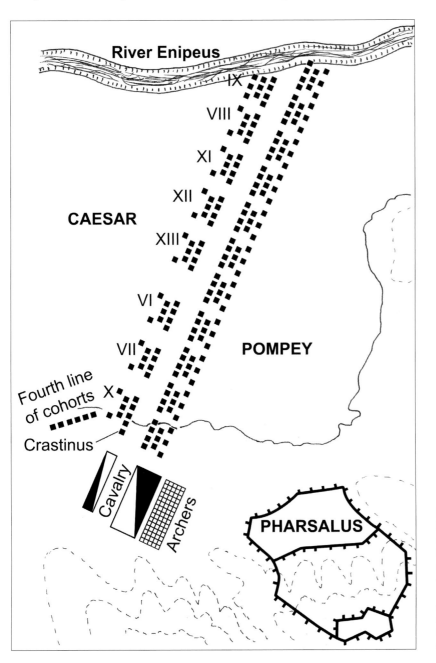

Battle of Pharsalus, 48 BC. Note Caesar's oblique fourth line of cohorts, assembled by weakening the third line, concealed behind the cavalry and *legio X*. Crastinus and his 'forlorn hope' of volunteers occupy the position of honour at the extreme right of the infantry line. (Author's drawing, after Veith, 1906)

charge as soon as the infantry lines engaged. They were to smash through Caesar's puny force of 1,000 troopers and a few lightly equipped legionaries, surround his right wing and attack from the rear; Pompey thus hoped to catch Caesar in a devastating pincer movement.

Caesar discerned Pompey's plan to outflank him as soon as he saw the cavalry and light troops massed opposite his right wing. He withdrew six cohorts from the third battle line and formed them up in an oblique line behind the Tenth Legion, which held the right of the line, and the cavalry. He had effectively turned the army into a *quadruplex acies* – a quadruple battle line. The diminished third line was given strict orders not to engage until Caesar signalled it to do so by means of a *vexillum* banner.

The battle opened with the suicidal charge of Crastinus, the former *primus pilus* (senior centurion) of the Tenth Legion, and 120 volunteers who had served under him. This charge has the appearance of a *devotio*, a rite by which the gods of the Underworld were called upon to destroy the enemy, but which required human sacrifice – that is, the death in combat of whoever called upon the aid of the dark gods. Crastinus cut his way deep into the Pompeian ranks, but was killed when an enemy legionary thrust a *gladius* into his mouth with such force that the point emerged at the back of the centurion's neck.

The first and second Caesarian lines then charged at their customary run, but halted, caught their breath and redressed their line when they realized that the Pompeians were not counter-charging (Pompey had hoped that the Caesarians would be exhausted by having to charge twice the distance). It was their many years of combat experience that allowed them to do this without confusion; Caesar states that the halt was spontaneous, not resulting from an oral command (how could the whole line all hear such an order and act on it simultaneously?) or a trumpet signal. Just before they collided with the enemy, Caesar's men threw their *pila* and set to with swords; but the Pompeians, reinforced with 2,000 tough *evocati* veterans specially recalled by Pompey, threw their *pila* and evidently took the steam right out of the Caesarians' assault. A successful running charge would usually force the enemy back, but on this occasion Pompey's front line stood fast and held formation.

Pompey now let loose his cavalry, followed by the archers. Caesar's cavalry retreated before them, and the massed Pompeian horse divided into individual *turmae* to turn the flank of Caesar's third line of cohorts. At this point Caesar signalled his fourth line forward, taking the enemy cavalry completely by surprise; expecting to turn and slaughter legionaries from the rear, the Pompeians were confronted by a new battle line running furiously towards them. The leading *turmae* panicked and made to retreat, but presumably collided with the unsuspecting squadrons still coming around the flank. The legionaries did not throw their *pila*; Caesar had ordered them to use the weapons to thrust at the faces of the cavalrymen, since that would help spread the panic and add to the confusion.

Pompey's great force of cavalry was thus driven back by perhaps 1,650 legionaries. As the troopers scattered, Caesar's fourth line advanced to slaughter the now unprotected archers, and proceeded to assault the left wing of the Pompeian line in the flank and rear. Caesar now judged that it was time to bring his diminished third line of cohorts into action; on the pre-arranged signal these units came up and replaced the exhausted troops of the first and second lines. Attacked by fresh troops at the front, and with their second and third lines being savaged from the left and rear (Pompey may already have moved his reserve lines forward), the Pompeians buckled, turned and fled. Caesar claims that 15,000 Pompeians were killed and 24,000 surrendered, while he lost only 200 men – 30 of them 'strong, brave centurions'. However, Asinius Pollio, one of Caesar's legates at the battle, later refuted this, stating that Pompey lost 6,000 dead (Caes. *BC* 3.84–99; App. *BC* 2.75–82, quoting Pollio; Plut. *Pomp.* 69–72; Front. *Strat.* 2.3.22).

Was the spark of this victory provided by Crastinus' *devotio*? After the battle Caesar said that he was in Crastinus' debt, awarded him posthumous decorations, and built him a hero's tomb on the battlefield (Caes. *BC* 3.99; App. *BC* 2.82).

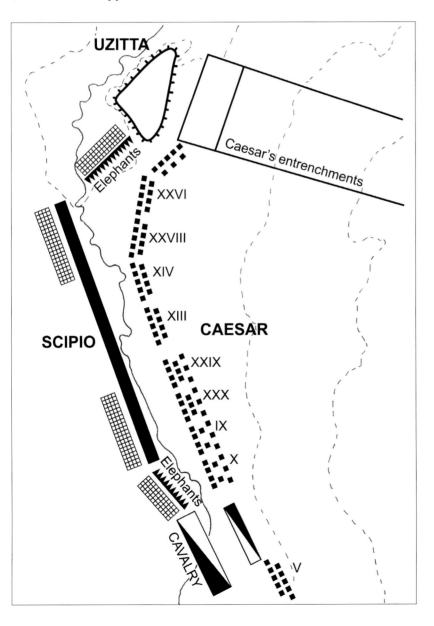

Caesar's battle line at Uzitta, 46 BC; (see text page 30). Note *triplex acies* on the left, but *duplex acies* on the right. (Author's drawing, after Kromayer & Veith, 1912)

During the operations at **Uzitta (46 BC)**, Caesar deployed his army in *triplex acies* against the combined armies of the senior Pompeian general Metellus Scipio and his ally, King Juba of Numidia. Scipio's and Juba's legions formed the main battle line, with a long, thin line of Numidians in reserve, and light infantry and war elephants on either flank. Before Juba arrived to reinforce him, Scipio led out his forces in what is described as his customary deployment, a *qudruplex acies*, the front line being composed of cavalry *turmae*, with war elephants between the *turmae* on the left and right flanks; but we are not told about the composition of the other three battle lines.

As the left wing of Scipio's infantry extended to the edge of the town of Uzitta, his cavalry were massed at the right. Caesar's cavalry formed on the left as a counter, while the right wing of his army was secured by entrenchments. Caesar's infantry lines was part *triplex*, and part *duplex acies*. His veteran legions at the left and centre of the line were in *triplex acies* because their left flank was exposed and they would bear the full brunt of the assault of the massed Pompeian cavalry; the new legions on the right were in *duplex acies* because their flank was secured by entrenchments. However, the Cesarian right still had to face a corps of war elephants, so Caesar reinforced the new legions with some cohorts detached from the second line of the veteran legions. Neither triplex nor duplex acies was put to the test, though. A cavalry battle ensued, which Caesar's over-eager troopers lost, but there was no general engagement. (Anon. *BAfr.* 41, 59–61).

The use of entrenchments was not unusual in Roman battles. Sulla used trenches at Orchomenus (86 BC), not only to protect the flanks of his army, but also to enclose the best ground and force the Pontic cavalry into marshland (Plut. *Sulla* 21.1). When fighting the younger Mithridates at the **River Rhyndacus (85 BC)**, Flavius Fimbria constructed two fortified lines of earthworks running out from his camp towards the enemy position, and linked at the far end by a ditch. The Roman army remained quietly within its fortifications; the Pontic prince, believing that they had lost the will to fight, sent his cavalry over the ditch and into the confines of the flanking fortifications. The Pontic attack was met with a sudden sortie (*eruptio*) from the Roman camp, and, unable to turn and retreat, some 6,000 cavalrymen were killed (Front. *Strat.* 3.17.5).

* * *

Caesar again used a variation of the *triplex acies* when he finally brought the Pompeians to battle at **Thapsus (46 BC)**. Scipio's war elephants were formed in front of the wings of his infantry and cavalry. To strengthen his array, Caesar placed five cohorts of *legio V Alaudae* in front of the wings facing the elephants. His legionary infantry may then have been in *quadruplex acies*, with a projecting first line, on the left and right, but it seems more likely that the fourth lines formed by the Fifth legion were on either side of the *triplex acies*, reinforcing the archers and slingers (Anon. *BAfr.* 81–84).

The battle started before Caesar wished, when the veteran legionaries on the right wing grew impatient and intimidated a *tubicen* (a trumpeter, responsible for sounding tactical signals) into blowing the call for 'attack'. The *triplex acies* on the right surged forward; Caesar accepted the situation, and gave the signal for the rest of the army to follow. The archers and slingers on the right loosed their missiles against the elephants on Scipio's left, who turned under this stinging hail and crashed back through their own lines. Scipio's Mauretanian cavalry on the far end of this flank turned and fled now that the protective wall of elephants had disappeared. The right Caesarian *triplex acies* swept over the ramparts of Scipio's lightly defended camp, which was immediately behind where his left wing had been: the Pompeians now had nowhere safe to retreat to. The Mauretanians' departure was the final straw that triggered the general flight of the rest of Scipio's army, but there was some fighting on the other wing:

> On the [Caesarean] left wing an elephant, maddened by the pain of a wound, had attacked an unarmed camp follower, pinned him underfoot and then knelt upon him. With its trunk aloft and

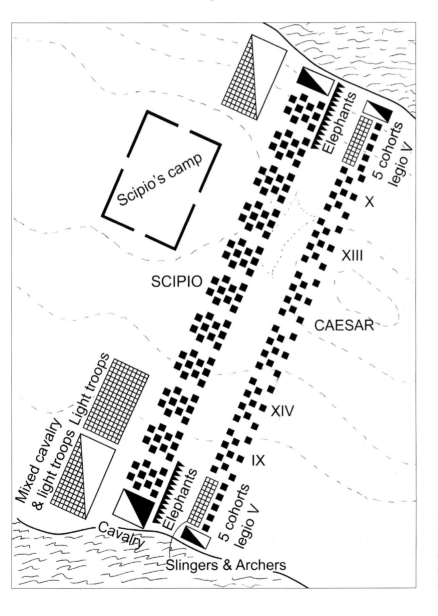

Battle of Thapsus, 46 BC. Scipio placed his hopes on his war elephants, but these were put to flight by Caesar's light missile troops and *legio V*. (Author's drawing, after Veith, 1906)

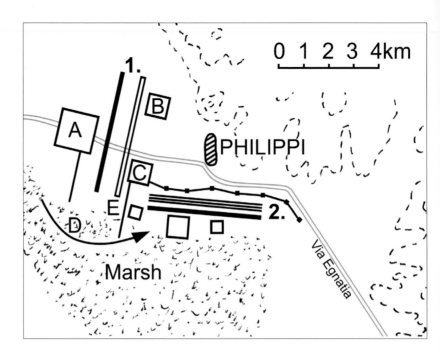

Battles of Philippi, 42 BC.
(1) First battle: (A) camp of Antony and Octavian; (B & C) camps of Brutus and Cassius; (D) Antony's attempt to outflank Cassius, (E) Cassius' countermove.
(2) Second battle: note Brutus' *triplex acies*. (Author's drawing, after Keppie, 1984)

trumpeting loudly, it was crushing the man to death. This was more than a veteran of the Fifth Legion could endure and, fully armed as he was, he attacked the beast. When the elephant became aware of him advancing with weapon ready to strike, it abandoned the corpse of the camp follower, encircled the veteran with its trunk and lifted him off the ground. The veteran, realizing that this dangerous crisis required determination on his part, hacked with his *gladius* at the encircling trunk with all his strength. The resulting pain caused the elephant to drop the veteran, turn about and, trumpeting shrilly, swiftly rejoin its fellow beasts (Anon., *African War* 84).

After the battle the elephant was adopted as the emblem of *legio V Alaudae* (App. *BC* 2.96).

* * *

The second battle of **Philippi (42 BC)** in Macedonia again saw a Roman army formed in a *triplex acies*, but the formation did not lead to victory. Marcus Junius Brutus (assassin of Caesar, and leader of the Republican cause) drew up his legions in three lines, presumably on the 4-3-3 cohort arrangement, though our sources do not make this clear. The array of the Caesarian army, led by Mark Antony and Octavian, is not known (these Caesarian leaders had been reconciled in 43 BC following the battles at Forum Gallorum and Mutina). At the first battle of Philippi, some three weeks before, Antony, on the right, routed Cassius' division of the Republican army; but in the second battle Plutarch tells us that Brutus' army was defeated first on its left wing, i.e. by the Caesarian right; the victorious Caesarian legionaries are identified by Appian (who does not, however, specify the wing) as belonging to Octavian.

(continued on page 41)

LEGIONARY CENTURIES IN CLOSE AND OPEN ORDER
See text commentary for details

O & T

O

T

C Tr S

Tr

C

S

O

T

Tr

C S

THE *TESTUDO*
See text commentary for details

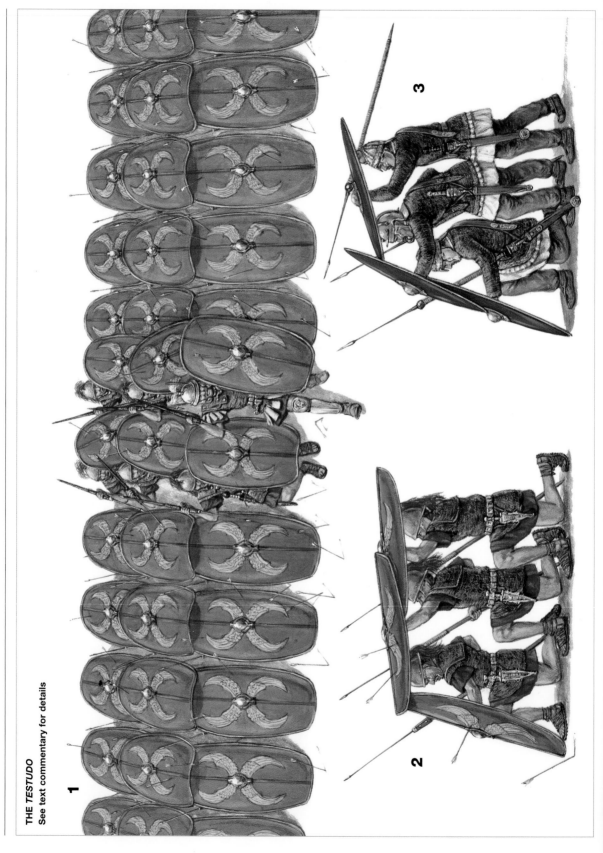

1

2

3

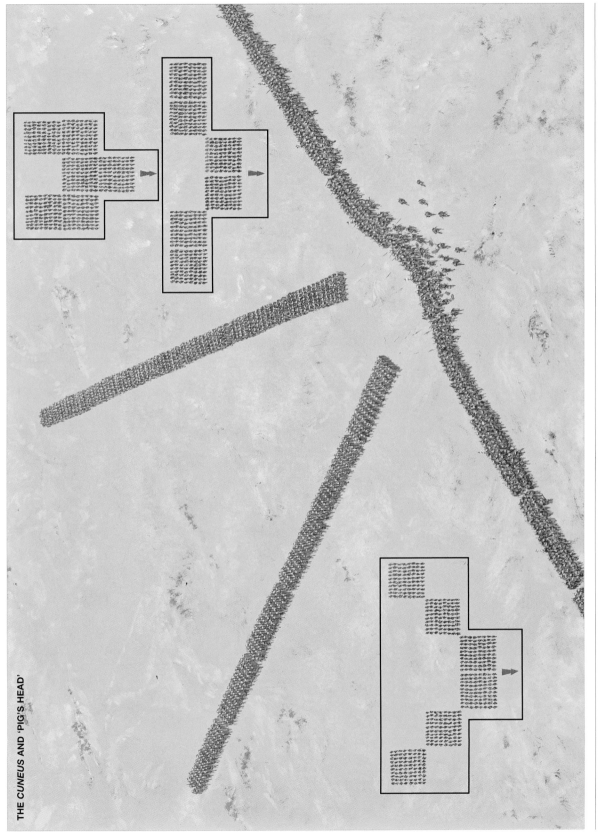

THE *CUNEUS* AND 'PIG'S HEAD'

c

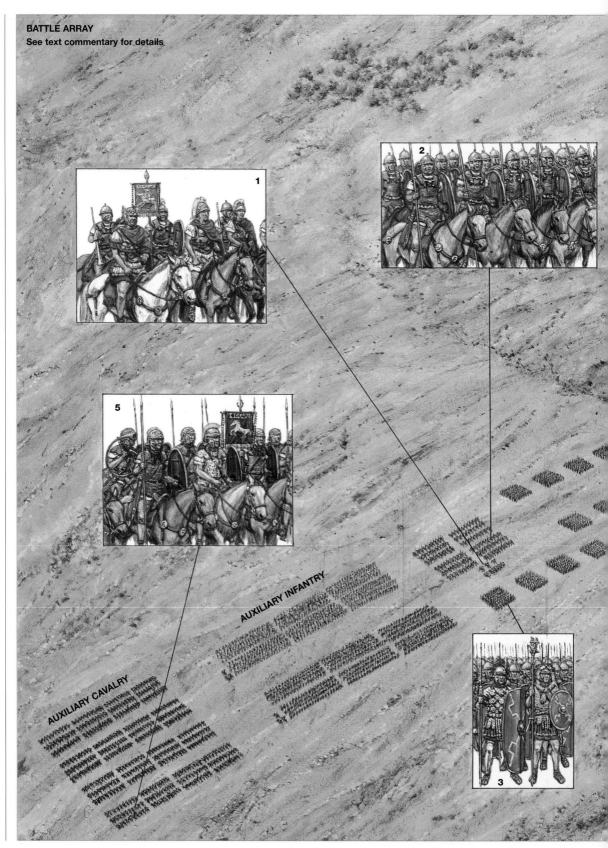

BATTLE ARRAY
See text commentary for details

AUXILIARY INFANTRY

AUXILIARY CAVALRY

D

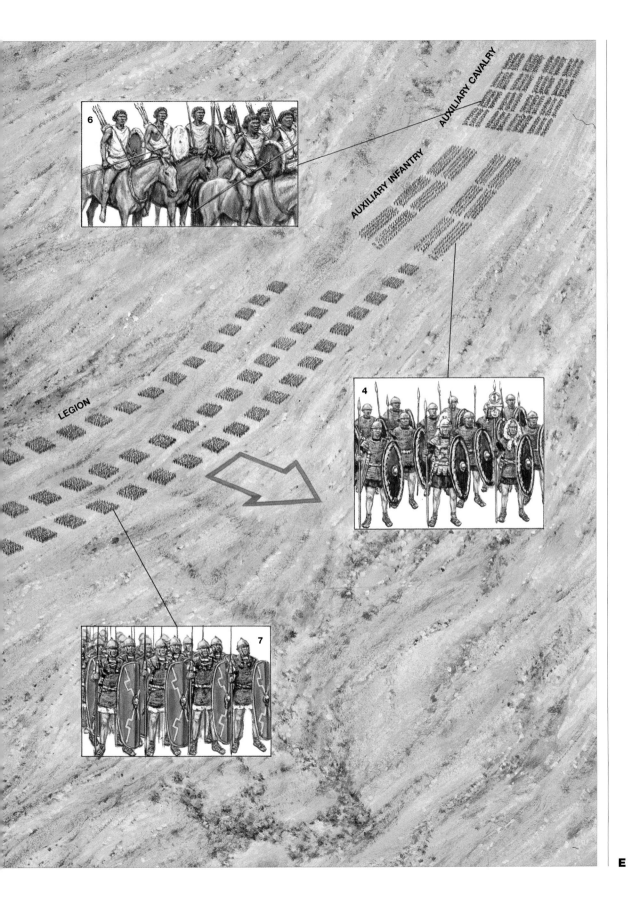

AUXILIARY CAVALRY

AUXILIARY INFANTRY

6

4

LEGION

7

LEGIONARY CENTURY CHARGING
See text commentary for details

F

LANCIARII ATTACKING
PARTHIAN CATAPHRACTS
See text commentary for details

G

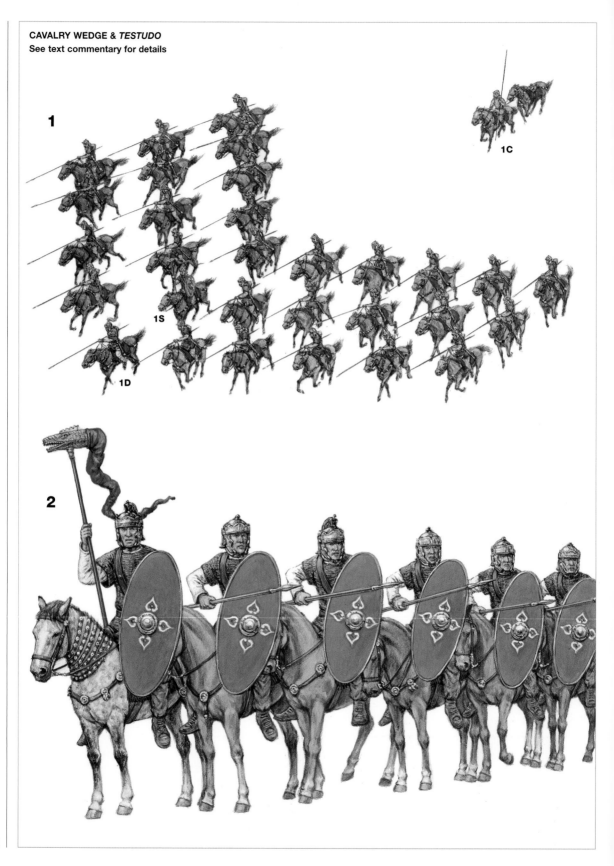

1

1C

1S

1D

2

Appian's account of the battle is of a purely frontal, head-on collision of legions. As in his description of Forum Gallorum, 'the bodies of the fallen were carried back and others stepped into their places from the reserves'; but the battle finally turned in the Caesarians' favour when Octavian's legionaries forced back Brutus' first battle line, 'as though they were turning round a heavy machine' – which suggests a wheeling movement. At first the Republican legionaries fell back step by step, but orderly retreat soon dissolved into full-scale flight. As the first line ran, the men in the second and third lines did not hold firm but also turned on their heels. The fugitives of the first line ran into those of the second, and they into the third: the Republican *triplex acies* became a disorganized mass (App. *BC* 4.128).

Plutarch's description of the battle makes no mention of Brutus' *triplex acies*, and offers more complex reasons for the collapse of the Republicans. Commanding the right of the battle line, Brutus succeeded in defeating the Caesarian left and put it to flight; but the Republican left was itself hard pressed by the superior numbers of the enemy. Those in command of the wing gave the order to extend line to prevent envelopment, but the thinning ranks could not resist the pressure of the deeper Caesarian formations. It was at this point that the Republican legionaries on the left turned and fled. The Caesarian right did not pursue but wheeled their line to hammer into Brutus' now exposed left flank (Plut. *Brut.* 49.5–7).

The *triplex acies* is absent from the battle descriptions of the early Empire but, as already mentioned, the sources for the Imperial period are usually vague when it comes to the fine details of deployment in battle. It is entirely possible that the *triplex acies* gradually fell out of general use, for it was best suited to large legionary armies, and not all battles were on the same scale as Pharsalus. One might assume that the formation was still widely employed during the Augustan conquests, i.e. while the generals of Augustus (the name Octavian took when he became the first emperor) were veterans of the civil wars in which the *triplex acies* had played such a decisive role.

Detached forces and surprise attacks

When Licinius Lucullus won his famous victory at **Tigranocerta (69 BC)** he had 24 cohorts – that is, two complete legions and another four legionary cohorts – totalling 10,000 men. His combined force of cavalry, archers and slingers numbered only 1,000. Ranged against Lucullus was the immense army of Tigranes, king of Armenia: reportedly, 55,000 cavalry, 17,000 of which were heavily armoured cataphract lancers; 10,000 archers and slingers; 150,000 infantry, and 35,000 engineers, smiths and other specialists. No doubt these figures are hugely exaggerated, as was the norm in ancient sources, but it is clear that Lucullus' small army was greatly outnumbered (the principal sources for Tigranocerta are Plut. *Luc.* 26–28 and App. *Mith.* 85).

Lucullus marched towards the enemy in line of battle, presumably a *simplex acies* in order to present as broad a front as possible to an opponent so strong in cavalry. When his line of advance was obstructed by a river, the legionary cohorts wheeled into a column and each cohort divided into individual maniples or centuries to make the crossing. When Tigranes saw the Romans begin their manoeuvre he thought they

Portrait bust associated with Lucullus, the victor at Tigranocerta (69 BC). Despite being massively outnumbered by the Armenians, his personal leadership of a detached force of just two cohorts in a surprise attack secured a remarkable triumph. A stern disciplinarian, who lacked the charisma of a Sulla or a Caesar, Lucullus was never a popular commander, but he earned his soldiers' respect by leading by example. The overconfident King Tigranes had not believed that the Romans would dare to fight him at such odds, and had quipped to his entourage, 'If they come as ambassadors, they are too many; if they come as soldiers, they are too few!' (RHC Archive)

were in the process of turning about, and poured scorn on them for retreating. However, the Romans forded the river and came on, and his minister Taxiles, evidently knowledgeable in Roman battle customs, said to the king:

When these men are merely on the march, they do not put on gleaming armour, nor have their shields polished and helmets uncovered, as they have now taken the leather covers from their armour. No, this splendour means they are going to fight, and are now advancing on their enemies (Plutarch, *Lucullus* 27.5).

(In his account of the battle of the Sabis, Caesar remarks that the surprise attack of the Belgae left his men no time to affix their *insignia* – helmet crests and feathers which identified the wearer with the war god Mars – and military decorations (Caes. *BG* 2.21; Virg. *Aen.* 6.779). Decorations and fine equipment were not reserved for parades; they were displayed in battle as a mark of the wearer's prowess and pride, so this detail from Plutarch's account emphasizes that Lucullus' legionaries really did mean business.)

The Romans formed up opposite Tigranes' right wing, which was protected on its flank by a hill, and the majority of the cataphracts were arrayed in front of the main battle line. Lucullus prepared to make a running charge, a typical Roman method of minimizing the time during which legionaries would be exposed to arrows and sling bullets before they closed with the enemy (cf Front. *Strat.* 2.2.5, for Ventidius' tactics against the Parthians; Dio 37.2.3, for Pompey versus Asiatic Iberian archers). However, at the last moment the general decided to change his tactics, and ordered his few *turmae* of Gallic and Thracian cavalry to harass the flank of the cataphracts. While the attention of the cataphracts was distracted by this diversion, Lucullus led a detached force of two legionary cohorts at the run up the far side of the hill that was supposed to protect the flank of Tigranes' battle line.

It was an exhausting climb, but the legionaries were encouraged that their general led the way on foot and wearing full armour. The summit of the hill was flat; Lucullus paused there momentarily, not just to rest his legionaries, but to allow the enemy to see them and understand that their flank had been turned. Yelling 'The day is ours, fellow soldiers!', Lucullus sprinted down the hill with the two cohorts racing behind him. Plutarch relates the result of Lucullus' audacious tactics:

The cataphracts did not wait for the Romans, but, with loud cries and in most disgraceful flight, they hurled themselves and their horses upon the ranks of their own infantry, before it had so much as begun to fight, and so all those tens of thousands were defeated without the infliction of a wound or the sight of blood. The great slaughter began at once when they fled, or rather tried to flee, for they were prevented from doing so by the closeness and depth of their own ranks. Tigranes rode away at the very onset with a few attendants, and took to flight... It is said that more than 100,000 of the enemy's infantry perished, while of the cavalry only a few, all told, made their escape. Of the Romans only 100 were wounded, and only five killed... They were almost ashamed, and laughed one another to scorn for requiring arms against such slaves (Plutarch, *Lucullus* 28.5–7).

As always, we may dismiss these figures as ridiculous, while still accepting that a surprising victory had been won with hugely disproportionate losses.

The Romans frequently used detached forces to surprise opponents in the flank or rear. The night before the second day of fighting at **Aquae Sextiae (102 BC)**, Gaius Marius sent his lieutenant, Claudius Marcellus, with 3,000 heavy infantry to circle round to the rear of the army of the Teutones, conceal themselves in the hilly terrain, then attack the enemy from behind when the battle was rejoined. (It is worth noting here that Marcellus' heavy infantry may not have been legionaries but were perhaps drawn from the allied Italian cohorts; it was not until 88 BC, and following the horrors of the Social War – *socii*, 'allies' – that Roman citizenship, and with it legionary status, was granted to the Italian cities and tribes that supplied half or more of the manpower of the Roman army.)

Marius was camped on a hill and drew up his army before the rampart; the number of lines in his array is not recorded. The Teutones were forced to advance uphill, and were welcomed with a volley of *pila*. Marius wanted the Germans to be bunched together, unable to manoeuvre or wield their weapons properly. This was accomplished by shoving the leading warriors back with shield and sword blows, while the Germans at the rear of the formation were still trying to press on. When the pressure from the rear of the crowd finally eased the Teutones – half-willingly, half under force of

Battle scene from Trajan's Column, early 2nd century AD: Roman auxiliaries advance on a Dacian fort, stepping over the bodies of the fallen. The Dacian formation is breaking, and the rearmost warriors flee inside the stockade. Again, unarmoured allied tribesmen with the lightest of weapons are shown on the flank of the Roman shield wall, and note that the heavy infantry are backed by a rank of archers, shown here in tall helmets and flowing tunics. (RHC Archive)

Auxiliary slingers of the late 2nd century AD, depicted on the Column of Marcus Aurelius. These light troops appear to be using stones as missiles, but cast lead bullets were also common – and deadly. At Mount Gindarus in 38 BC the slingers of Ventidius' army drove Parthian heavy cavalry and horse archers back during a downhill charge. (RHC Archive)

circumstance – retreated down the hill on to level ground. The Germans' leading ranks took the opportunity to re-form the battle line, but their rear ranks were in complete disarray. It was now that Marcellus appeared:

Marcellus had waited for his opportunity, and when the cries of battle were carried up over the hills, he charged with his men at the run and fell with loud shouts on the enemy's rear, where he cut down the hindmost of them. Those in the rear forced along those who were in front of them, and quickly plunged the whole army into confusion, and under this double attack they could not hold out for long, but broke ranks and fled (Plutarch, *Marius* 21.1–2).

It is unfortunate that Plutarch's account does not identify Marcellus' attack formation; perhaps his force was in a *simplex acies*, so that he could engage as great a width as possible of the Teutones' compressed formation. That his men shouted warcries as they attacked was a standard feature of Roman warfare; Julius Caesar considered warcries and shouting essential for the morale of an army and to intimidate the enemy (Caes. *BC* 3.92). For the same reason the Romans might also drum swords or *pila* against their shields, as Pompey's legionaries did in the victory over Mithridates of Pontus in Armenia in 66 BC (Dio 36.49.1). The opposing legionaries at Philippi (42 BC) clashed weapons as they advanced on each other; and Antony's legionaries and praetorians did so while charging Parthian cavalry at Phraata in 36 BC (Dio 47.43.2–3; Plut. *Ant.* 39.4).

Pompey the Great was the victim of a surprise attack on his rear at **Lauron (76 BC)**. His opponent, the Roman rebel Sertorius, withdrew from his camp at Pompey's approach and took up position on a nearby hill. Pompey was pleased, thinking he could besiege Sertorius' army; but as he advanced up the hill, 6,000 soldiers that Sertorius had hidden in the apparently abandoned camp moved to attack him from behind. A shamefaced Pompey managed to withdraw before he was trapped; this episode demonstrates that even great generals could be caught out by simple tactics (Plut. *Sert.* 18.3–5).

Caecilius Metellus Pius, Pompey's fellow commander in the same war, was jeered by his own soldiers when he refused Sertorius' challenge to single combat; Metellus was of the mind that 'a general should die like a general, not like a common soldier' (Plut. *Sert.* 13.3–4). He certainly demonstrated his skill as a general the following year in the battle against Sertorius' lieutenant, Hirtuleius, at **Segovia (75 BC)**. Metellus was informed that Hirtuleius had positioned his best cohorts in the centre of his line. Perhaps inspired by the strategy that had allowed Hannibal to destroy a Roman army at Cannae (Polyb. 3.113–117; Livy 22.43–51), Metellus drew back the centre of his line, so that it would not engage Hirtuleius' best troops immediately. While the troops on the wings engaged, Hirtuleius' centre kept on advancing, but the weaker cohorts on his wings were defeated by Metellus' men, who proceeded to envelop and completely surround the centre of Hirtuleius' *acies* (Front. *Strat.* 2.3.5).

Downhill and uphill charges

In 39 and 38 BC the Parthians invaded Roman Syria, but were soundly defeated by Mark Antony's lieutenant, Ventidius Bassus. Learning from Crassus' disastrous tactics at Carrhae, Ventidius offered battle on high ground at **Mount Amanus (39 BC)**, and when the over-confident Parthian cataphracts charged directly up the slope he simply counter-charged down the slope with his infantry at the run. The leading Parthian ranks were thrown back in confusion by the force and speed of the assault, and as Ventidius' legionaries and light troops assailed them with missiles and swords they attempted to turn and retreat; but other Parthian squadrons were still coming up from behind, and their ranks dissolved into a chaotic mass (Dio 48.40.1–3).

In this memorial carving Ares (left), a legionary of the later 2nd century AD, offers his sword, shield and helmet to the war god Mars. (In the British Museum; author's photo)

In 38 BC Ventidius did not oppose the Parthian army as it crossed the River Euphrates, but remained in his camp on the slopes of **Mount Gindarus**. The Parthians took this inaction as a sign of weakness and advanced on the camp; however, they had learned from the rout at Mount Amanus, and the cataphracts were now supported by horse archers. The Romans again made a sudden running charge (over 500 paces, claims Frontinus) in order to minimize their time 'under fire', and the legionaries slammed into the horsemen, driving the leading ranks back down the slope and reducing the assault formation to disarray. Ventidius' slingers (*funditores*) followed up, their heavy lead bullets (*glandes*) bringing down armoured cataphracts and horse archers – whose bows they easily outranged – with equal ease. When the Parthian crown prince Pacorus fell his retainers fought desperately to recover his body, but when they were also slain the rest of the Parthian troopers gave up the hellish uphill struggle and fled back to the Euphrates (Dio 49.20.1–3; Front. *Strat.* 2.2.5).

The tactical advantages of holding a position allowing a downhill charge are obvious; and mention has already been made, in some of the previous accounts in this text, of the problems of advancing and charging up slopes. Nevertheless, Roman armies won some notable victories by fighting their way uphill.

After being pinned down for five hours on the steep approach to **Ilerda (49 BC)**, three cohorts of the Ninth Legion drew their swords – their supply of *pila* being long exhausted – and made a desperate charge up the slope to scatter the surprised Pompeians (Caes. *BC* 1.46). The Ninth made another successful uphill charge the following year at **Dyrrhachium** (*ibid.* 3.46). Mark Antony led that charge; and perhaps with its success in mind, he overwhelmed Cassius' outer works and camp at the first battle of **Philippi (42 BC)** by making an audacious uphill advance. This attack was all the more extraordinary in that it was accomplished at the run, the legionaries being burdened with ladders and tools, and the line of advance was oblique (App. *BC* 4.111). Finally, the advance made by the Batavian and Tungrian auxiliary cohorts up the side of **Mons Graupius (AD 84)** carried them so deep into the ranks of the Caledonians that they were temporarily enveloped (Tac. *Agric.* 36–37).

OFFENSIVE AND DEFENSIVE FORMATIONS

The *cuneus* and 'pig's head'

The *cuneus* was a dense formation employed for crashing through thin battle lines, or exploiting gaps in formations. *Cunei* were used to devastating effect by the rebel Batavian cohorts against the disorderly *simplex acies* of *legio I Germanica* and auxiliary cohorts at **Bonn (AD 69)**:

> Three thousand legionaries and some hastily raised cohorts of Belgic auxiliaries, as well as a band of country folk and camp followers – untrained, but bold before they met actual danger – all burst out of the fortress gates to surround the Batavi, who were inferior in numbers. But being veterans in military service, they formed into dense *cunei*, with their ranks closed on every side, secure on front, flanks and rear, and so they broke through our thin line. When the Belgic cohorts gave way, the legion was driven back and in terror fled for the rampart and gates of the fortress. Here the greatest casualties were suffered; the ditches were piled high with bodies, and our men were killed not only by the sword, but also by the crush and many by their own weapons (Tacitus, *Histories* 4.30).

In **Britain (AD 61)**, Suetonius Paulinus' outnumbered army formed up in a line of *cunei* against Boudicca's great host. Paulinus had *legio XIV*, a vexillation (detachment) of *legio XX*, and auxiliary infantry and cavalry. The total number of Roman troops was 10,000, set against Boudicca's horde – 230,000 warriors, according to Dio (62.8.2), and certainly vastly outnumbering the Romans. Like Catilina at Pistoria, Paulinus secured the flanks of his army by forming up in a defile, while a wood blocked the approach to his rear. The army was deployed in the typical manner, with the legionaries at the centre, auxiliary cohorts on either side, and the cavalry holding the wings:

> At first, the legionaries stood motionless, keeping to the natural defences of the defile; but when the enemy had advanced close enough to allow it they hurled their *pila* with accuracy until the supply of missiles was exhausted, and then erupted forwards in *cuneus* formations. The auxiliaries charged in the same manner, and the cavalry, with spears extended, broke through any resistance they encountered. The rest of the enemy turned and took to flight, but escape was difficult because their wagons blocked their route. The Romans gave no quarter even to the women, and speared the baggage animals and added them to the piles of dead. The glory won in the course of the day was remarkable, and equal to that of the victories of old. By some accounts just under 80,000 Britons were slain, while only 400 Romans fell (Tacitus, *Annals* 14.37).

The potency of the *cuneus* is clear, but what exactly was it? The Latin word means 'wedge'; but Tacitus' description of the Batavian *cunei* at Bonn does not suggest triangular formations, but formations with four sides – which is why translators of the passage normally render *cuneus* as 'square' or 'column'. Tacitus describes legionaries fighting in *cunei* at the first battle of **Cremona (AD 69)**, but there the term is used of those soldiers who could not form a regular extended battle line because of obstacles such as trees, ditches and vineyards in the agricultural landscape (*Hist.* 2.42). Tacitus' use of *cuneus* suggests that it was a term that could broadly be applied to any deep but narrow-fronted formation.

The Romans even applied the term to descriptions of the Macedonian phalanx (Livy 32.17.11). This, of course, was a very deep but wide linear formation, so this usage is puzzling. Perhaps *cuneus* actually applied to the individual units making up the phalanx. The basic unit of the Macedonian phalanx was the *speira* of 256 men arranged shoulder to shoulder in files of 16, and with a front of 16 men. Every phalangite was armed with the great *sarissa* pike, and block after block of *speirai* combined to form a seemingly impenetrable wall of iron

Early 2nd-century AD legionaries march across a bridge of boats to begin the Dacian campaign, on Trajan's Column. The trumpeters and standard-bearers (right) are distinguished by the pelts of animal heads over their helmets and shoulders; among the standards are examples of the *signum, vexillum, aquila* and those of praetorian units with multiple wreathed images. The legionaries (centre) march with shields and helmets slung, carrying their kit on T-shaped poles. The cargo boats (left) are a visual reminder of the importance of logistics in any campaign. (RHC Archive)

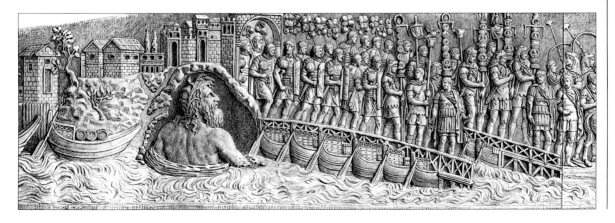

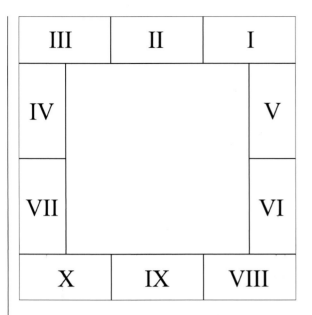

III	II	I
IV		V
VII		VI
X	IX	VIII

A legion of ten cohorts in *orbis* or *agmen quadratum* formation. The arrangement of cohort numbers indicates that the legion moved into this defensive formation from a *triplex acies* battle line. (Author's drawing)

pike heads. The Romans also viewed the manipular legion, with its individual maniples arranged at regular intervals in three lines, as forming rows of *cunei* (Front. *Strat.* 2.3.20). The *cunei* in the battle against Boudicca may therefore have been the individual cohorts or centuries in very close order (cf the legionary array in Plates D/E).

Vegetius says that late Roman soldiers nicknamed the *cuneus* the 'pig's head' (*caput porcinum*), and describes it as narrower at the front than it was at the rear. The name suggests that this kind of formation did not taper to a point but, like a pig's snout, had a flat front (see Plate C, insets); one imagines that a literally triangular formation would have its point rapidly blunted by enemy missiles. Vegetius adds the interesting details that the *cuneus* or 'pig's head' also allowed the missiles of as many soldiers as possible to bear on a single point of the enemy battle line, but that it was vulnerable to a counter-formation called the *forfex* ('forceps'), which was shaped like a V and could envelop the *cuneus* (Veg. *Epit.* 1.26, 3.17–19).

It has also been suggested that a wedge-like *cuneus* was achieved by two dense columns advancing obliquely at converging angles, so that the heads of the columns would meet, or nearly so, and strike the enemy battle line at the same point (Lammert 1940). Once the heads struck the enemy line, the two columns could swing forward like gates around this pivot, to fight as a regular line. Of course, such a tactic would also have had a huge psychological impact on those soldiers directly in its path; the *cuneus* would be vulnerable to volleys of missiles and to envelopment, but it would not be surprising if soldiers facing it lost their nerve before the actual physical impact (see Plate C, main image).

The *orbis*

Orbis means 'world' or 'circular' but, like the *cuneus*, when used of a formation the term was not necessarily literal. The *orbis* was usually formed in emergencies, when a unit or complete army was surrounded by the enemy, and it was clearly designed for all-round defence.

When Marius was marching towards **Cirta (105 BC)**, his army was surprised at dusk by the combined cavalry of Jugurtha and Bocchus, king of Mauretania. The enemy attacked 'not in orderly lines', wrote Sallust, 'but in swarms'. The Romans defended themselves as best they could, but as the marching column of foot and horse coalesced into disorganized masses the Africans surrounded the Roman army. Gradually, however, under the guidance of centurions and veterans, the groups formed into orderly *orbes*, 'thus at once protecting themselves on all sides and presenting an orderly front to the attacks of the enemy'. Using his bodyguard of picked cavalry, Marius aided the *orbes* under most pressure and, by hand signals – for vocal orders could not be heard over the din of combat – he eventually succeeded in co-ordinating a retreat to two nearby hills.

The following day, just before dawn, the Romans charged down from the hills, screaming warcries and with trumpets blaring. The Numidians and Mauretanians camped at the foot of the hills were too befuddled after a night of raucous celebrations to react to the unexpected assault; many were cut down, while the rest, including Jugurtha and Bocchus, scattered. Marius resumed his march, but in an *agmen quadratum* (hollow square or rectangle) formation (Sall. *BJug.* 97–101).

Some modern scholars have suggested that the *orbis* was in fact similar to the *agmen quadratum* – cf Crassus' formation at Carrhae; Vegetius refers to the hollow square as the *acies quadrata* – four-sided battle line (*Epit.* 1.26). It is perhaps easier to imagine the *orbis* formed by the legionaries of **Sabinus and Cotta in 54 BC**, when they were ambushed by treacherous Ambiorix and the Eburones, as roughly

Gravestone of Aelius Septimus (left), an *optio* of *legio I Adiutrix*, who was killed in a battle against the Naristae in AD 173 during the Danube campaign, during which the *orbis* was successfully employed against Sarmatian armoured cavalry. (RHC Archive)

square rather than circular. From this *orbis* individual cohorts made charges, but each time sustained heavy casualties from attacks to their exposed flanks, and the formation was gradually worn down (Caes. *BG* 5.33–35). Caesar's army at Ruspina also briefly formed into an *orbis* when it was surrounded, but there is no suggestion in that account that the line formed into a circle or square. It seems most likely that the *orbis* at Ruspina was achieved simply by the soldiers closing up together, while those on the flanks and in the rear made quarter- or half-turns where they stood so as to face the enemy (Anon. *BAfr.* 15).

Whatever its shape, the *orbis* could facilitate successful retreats, or enable soldiers to hold out against superior enemy forces for considerable lengths of time. During Caesar's first invasion of **Britain (55 BC)**, 300 legionaries were gradually surrounded by some 6,000 Morini warriors; but by forming an *orbis* they managed to fend the Morini off for four hours until Caesar's cavalry came to the rescue, and sustained remarkably few casualties (Caes. *BG*. 4.37).

In AD 16 the Roman-allied Batavian chief **Chariovalda** unwittingly led his men into a trap when pursuing Cherusci warriors, who feigned a retreat to draw him into a woodland clearing where he was surrounded. The Batavi formed an *orbis*, but suffered greatly from the repeated charges and missiles of the Germans. Chariovalda ordered his warriors to cut their way free in a *caterva* ('mass', in this instance perhaps similar to a *cuneus*). The break-out was only partially successful; Chariovalda and many of his nobles were killed, and some of the Batavi were extricated only when a relief force of Roman cavalry arrived (Tac. *Ann.* 2.11).

Sarmatian cataphracts depicted in retreat, in a famous scene from Trajan's Column; note how one rider has turned in the saddle to loose an arrow. The Sarmatian tribe who allied with the Dacians against the Romans in AD 101–102 were the Roxolani rather than the culturally similar Iazyges, but in the later Marcomannic Wars of AD 168–180 the Iazyges raided the provinces of Pannonia and Dacia. All Sarmatian heavy cavalry seem to have been similarly equipped, with *spangenhelm* helmets, and scale armour for man and horse – though not, obviously, as all-enveloping and form-fitting as shown by the Roman sculptor. (RHC Archive)

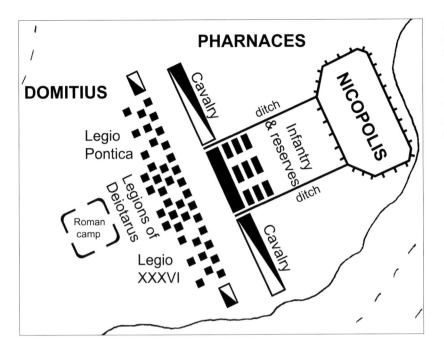

Battle of Nicopolis, 47 BC. Domitius' *legio XXXVI* was victorious on the right; but when the *legio Pontica* was repulsed and the legions of Deiotarus fled, it was forced to make a long retreat in *orbis* formation. (Author's drawing, after Veith, 1906)

The *orbis* enabled the Caesarian *legio XXXVI* to escape with minor casualties from a defeat at **Nicopolis (47 BC)** in Armenia Minor (Anon. *BAlex.* 38–40). Fighting the invading army of Pharnaces, king of Bosphorus (and son of Mithridates of Pontus), Domitius Calvinus had the experienced Thirty-Sixth Legion holding the right wing of his army, the locally recruited *legio Pontica* on the left, and two legions raised by Deiotarus, the king of Armenia Minor and Galatia, in the centre. However, Calvinus only allowed the Deiotarian legions a narrow frontage and most of their cohorts were held in reserve. Pharnaces' infantry were drawn up between two trenches dug to protect their flanks and extending as far forward as the king planned to advance, but all of his cavalry were stationed outside these trenches.

The opposing commanders gave the signal to charge almost simultaneously. *Legio XXXVI* cut through the cavalry facing it, swung in to cross one trench, and assaulted Pharnaces' infantry from the rear; but a similar manoeuvre by the *legio Pontica* failed, and many of its men were trapped in the trench covering Pharnaces' right. Meanwhile the Deiotarian legions had fled in the face of the assault by Pharnaces' infantry, and *legio XXXVI* found itself cut off:

> Victorious on their own right wing and at the centre of the line, the king's forces now turned on *legio XXXVI*. However, the legion bravely resisted the attack… and, despite being surrounded by large enemy forces, had the presence of mind to form an *orbis* and so made a fighting withdrawal to the foot of the mountains. Pharnaces was unwilling to pursue because of the steepness of the terrain. So, with the Pontic legion almost totally lost and a large proportion of the soldiers of Deiotarus killed, *legio XXXVI* retreated to higher ground with losses no greater than 250 men (Anon., *Alexandrian War* 40).

Legionaries in *testudo* formation approach an enemy fortification. Note the various missiles thrown down onto the roof of the formation – rocks, cartwheels, flaming brands, even pots of boiling oil or water. From the Column of Marcus Aurelius. (RHC Archive)

This retreat into the hills, accomplished under enemy pressure and without losing cohesion, was clearly no mean feat. In AD 9 the future emperor Tiberius arranged part of his army into a dense square formation (an *acies quadrata*?) to assault the Dalmatian hill fortress of **Andretium**. Even before the Dalmatians started lobbing missiles and rolling boulders down on the Romans, the square formation had broken up:

> They proceeded first at a walk, but then they became separated by the steepness and unevenness of the mountain, which was full of gullies and at many points was cut up into ravines, so that some climbed more rapidly and others more slowly (Dio 56.13.5).

Finally, the formation in which the Romans defeated the Sarmatian Iazyges on the frozen **River Danube** in the winter of AD 173/174 was presumably some form of *orbis* or *acies quadrata*. Pursued across the river, the Iazyges – all cavalry – halted on the thick ice and waited for the Romans to catch up; they had long experience of negotiating the ice, and expected to defeat the Romans on the treacherous surface. When the Romans got near the Iazyges attacked, some coming straight on, others moving to envelop the Romans' flanks. At this the Romans formed into a 'compact body that faced the enemy in every direction'. This close formation received the charge of the Iazyges with ease (it was presumably not at the speed usual for a charge on land), and soldiers scrambled forward to grab the horses' tack and haul riders from their saddles. The battle dissolved into a mêlée, with men and horses slipping and falling as they struggled on the ice. The Romans – who were apparently not above using even their teeth as they grappled with the enemy – prevailed (Dio 71.7; cf Livy 22.51.5–9 for mauling in combat).

The *testudo*

We have already encountered the *testudo* ('tortoise') at the battle of Carrhae. This archetypal Roman formation was widely employed in both sieges and pitched battles to protect soldiers from hails of missiles. The *testudo* could be formed by any number from a mere handful of soldiers – as at Saguntum in 75 BC, when legionaries surrounded the wounded Metellus and carried him to safety (Plut. *Sert.* 21.2) – to a complete army, such as Mark Antony's during the retreat from Media in 36 BC (see below). The interlocked roof of shields of a large and properly formed *testudo* was supposed to be strong enough for a horse-drawn chariot to be driven across it (Dio 49.39.3).

It was strongest when it was static, but was frequently employed for an advance on enemy fortifications or battle lines. When a *testudo* reached an enemy wall the formation could be sloped down by the ranks kneeling and stooping from the rear, thus forming an assault ramp, or at least reducing the distance to the top of the wall (Livy 44.9.6). The rebel Batavian cohorts used this tactic when attacking the legionary fortress of Vetera in AD 69 (Tac. *Hist.* 4.23).

At the battle of **Issus (AD 194)** the army of Pescennius Niger was formed high up in the Cilician Gates pass. His main battle line was composed of legionaries, but behind them were ranks of javelineers, stone-throwers and archers, 'so that the front ranks, fighting at close quarters, should hold back the enemy, while the others from a distance should bring their strength into play by hurling their missiles over the heads of those in front'. The opposing Severan army had a similar array, legionaries at the front and light troops following (perhaps both armies could be described as being in *duplex acies*), but they had to climb and endure bombardment. When they advanced into missile range the Severan legionaries formed *testudines*, and so eventually came to close quarters with Niger's line; but in the hand-to-hand fighting the Severans had the worst of it – no doubt weary from their advance, and still under a missile barrage from Niger's light troops. Lobbing their weapons downhill, Niger's javelineers and stone-throwers would have had the advantage over the Severan light troops. Sulla had used a similar tactic at Chaeronea (86 BC): the Pontic phalanx collapsed under the double pressure of the frontal assault of the legionaries, and the continual hail of javelins and fire arrows from the light troops positioned immediately behind the legions (Plut. *Sulla* 18.4–6).

At Issus a timely thunderstorm, driving rain into the faces of Niger's troops but only onto the backs of the Severans, lessened the resolve of Niger's men, and the cry went up in the Severan army that Jupiter had sent the storm to aid them. Modern readers might scoff at such a reaction, but divine intervention was very real to the Romans. The Severan legionaries redoubled their efforts, and the enemy began to fall back.

Testudo of the type described by Livy, acting not only as a defence from missiles during the approach to defended walls but also as a ramp for other assault troops to climb. Unless the soldiers were trained acrobats it seems unlikely that several successive ranks could have stood on each others' shoulders to reach the parapet, and the effect shown here could only have been achieved if this *testudo* somehow sheltered scaling ladders – which might be feasible? (RHC Archive)

Then the Severan cavalry – detached earlier in the day to find a way round Niger's position – slammed into the rear of his army, and this decided the day (Dio 74.7; cf Her. 3.7.3–6, for the Severans' employing the same cavalry tactic at Lugdunum in AD 197).

Returning to the *testudo*: while the emperor Aurelian was in pursuit of the Palmyrene general Zabdas, he found his route blocked by a substantial force of Palmyrenes occupying a hill above **Daphne (AD 272)**. Aurelian ordered his soldiers to form a *testudo*, advance straight up the hill and take the position: 'The *testudo* will shake off any missiles or stones thrown at it' (Zosimus 1.52). And so it did, on this occasion; but the *testudo* was not invulnerable, and could be dismantled by those who knew how – other Roman soldiers. Following their great victory at the second battle of **Cremona (AD 69)**, the Flavian legions moved on the Vitellian camp, determined to take it:

> The soldiers [of *legio XIII Gemina*], raising their shields above their heads, advanced on the rampart in a dense *testudo* formation. Both sides used typical Roman tactics. The Vitellian legionaries rolled down heavy stones, and when they had split and loosened the overlapped shields, they thrust at the *testudo* with lances and pikes until they broke up its close structure and hurled their dead and mangled foes to the ground with great slaughter (Tacitus, *Hist* 3.27).

For all their military professionalism, the Romans were superstitious; they both believed in, and solicited, divine intervention in battle. This is the 'Rain Miracle' depicted on the Aurelian column, which refers to an action in AD 172 beyond the Danube. In hot summer weather, a Roman force surrounded by Quadi warriors retreated into a close formation with locked shields, perhaps an orbis or testudo. After their direct attacks failed the Quadi were waiting for thirst and exhaustion to weaken the Romans, when a sudden torrential thunderstorm not only allowed the legionaries to fill their helmets with water, but caused a flash flood that swept many warriors away. Here a weird deity made of flowing water is shown sheltering mail-clad legionaries as enemy warriors and their horses are drowned. (Petersen, Die Marcus-Säule, 1886)

The *agmen quadratum* and *testudo*

In 36 BC Mark Antony invaded the Parthian empire in a long-delayed mission to avenge Carrhae. (Julius Caesar had been preparing for the war when he was assassinated in March 44 BC by Brutus, Cassius and the other 'Liberators'.) But Antony was deserted en route by his Armenian allies, whose cataphracts and horse archers he had hoped to employ to contain the Parthian cavalry; his siege train and two legions were surrounded by the complete Parthian field army, and destroyed. Without the means to capture cities and running out of supplies, Antony decided to retreat from Media back into Armenia. The retreat lasted 27 days, during which time his army fought 18 battles against the Parthian pursuit force of 40,000 cataphracts and horse archers. Despite the length of the retreat, Antony held his army together by using the *agmen quatratum* and *testudo* formations, and by expanding on the tactics successfully used against the Parthians by Ventidius Bassus two years before.

As he retreated, Antony used his slingers, javelineers and cavalry in combination against the enemy. Whenever the Parthian cavalry threatened his battle lines or *agmen quadratum*, the slingers and light troops would sally out through the intervals in the formation and bombard them. While the Parthians were so occupied, Antony's predominantly Gallic cavalry would mass together, charge and scatter the enemy, but – unlike Publius Crassus at Carrhae – they did not pursue them far. The light troops and cavalry would withdraw and the smarting Parthians would turn and pursue, only to find themselves being drawn into range of the massed *pila* of the legionaries.

These tactics worked well until the fifth day of the retreat, when Flavius Gallus, the commander of the light troops and cavalry at the rear of the *agmen quadratum*, refused to withdraw in the face of the enemy, believing that he could rout the Parthians in hand-to-hand combat. Ignoring the pleas of his officers to retreat while they still could, he was gradually surrounded. The legionary commanders at the rear of the *agmen* then sent troops to relieve him, but instead of advancing the complete rear line they sent out only a few cohorts at a time, and these were defeated piecemeal. It was only the arrival of Antony with *legio III Gallica* from the front of the *agmen* that prevented a complete rout. The legion advanced through the Roman fugitives and presented an orderly battle line to the Parthians before they could charge into the disordered rear of the square.

The Parthians were encouraged by this success – Gallus' misjudgement had cost 3,000 Roman dead and 5,000 wounded – and attacked on the following days with vigour. The Romans reverted to their own hit-and-withdraw tactics; but when the *agmen quadratum* had to negotiate a steep descent and its progress was reduced to the slowest pace, the Parthian horse archers loosed volley after volley into the square. Antony sounded the halt and gave the order for a *testudo* to be formed (see Plate B):

The legionaries wheeled about [i.e. those on the flanks and rear of the square, so as to face outwards], enclosing the lighter armed troops within their ranks, while they themselves dropped on one knee and held out their shields before them. The second ranks held their shields up over the heads of the first, and the next rank likewise. (The resulting appearance is very much like a roof, it is an impressive sight, and is the most effective protection against arrows, which glance off it.) The Parthians, thinking that the Romans dropping on one knee was a sign of fatigue and exhaustion, put away their bows, grasped their lances by the middle and charged to close quarters. But the Romans, with a full battle cry, suddenly sprang up, and thrusting with their *pila* slew the foremost of the Parthians and put all the rest to flight. This happened also on the following days as the Romans, little by little, proceeded on their way (Plutarch, *Antony* 45.2–3).

The emperor Severus Alexander (r.AD 222–235), who was doomed by his defeat at the hands of King Ardashir in AD 233, when the Sassanians managed to destroy a *testudo* or *agmen quadratum* formation. He was already despised by the soldiery for his effeminacy, and his failure during the Persian war caused burning resentment. When in AD 235 he tried to avoid a war against the Alamanni – an emerging Germanic confederacy – by paying them a subsidy, he was lynched by legionary recruits, and the general Maximinus was hailed as emperor. (RHC Archive)

The Parthians eventually gave up attempts to come to close quarters with the Romans and simply harassed them with showers of arrows, especially at the rear of the marching square. The enemy did make one last major attempt to break the Roman formation as it was about to cross a river, but again the light troops sallied out, while the legionaries at the rear formed *testudo* (presumably retaining intervals for the light troops to retreat into), and the Parthians declined to assault it. Meanwhile Antony saw to it that his wounded were first to cross the river and drink – hunger and thirst were now the main enemies of the Romans, accounting for half of Antony's losses; then he came up with all the cavalry to act as a screen while the infantry crossed. The Parthians did not attack; close as they were to the border with Armenia, they unstrung their bows and saluted the Romans. Six days after this – the eighteenth battle of the retreat – the Romans were back in friendly territory (Plut. *Ant.* 41-50; Dio 49.24–31).

More than 260 years after Antony's abortive invasion of Parthia another Roman army advanced eastwards, making for Ctesiphon, now capital of the Sassanian Persian empire. The Sassanians had overthrown their Parthian overlords in c.AD 224, and almost immediately declared their intention to seize Rome's eastern provinces. Mesopotamia was overrun in AD 229; the Romans reconquered the province in AD 231, and in **AD 233** sent three armies into Persian territory to extract revenge. One army, following Antony's route from Armenia into Media, caused chaos. A second followed the Euphrates towards Ctesiphon (just south of modern Baghdad), expecting to rendezvous on the way with a third army under the command of the emperor Severus Alexander, but he failed to leave Roman Mesopotamia. The Sassanian king, Ardashir, abandoned attempts to contain the Romans in the north, and gathered his forces (the usual cataphracts and horse archers) for an all-out attack on the second invading army. Ardashir found the Romans completely unprepared, and surrounded them. A *testudo* was formed but it did not save the Romans:

Under missile attack from all sides, the Roman soldiers were destroyed, because they were unable to stand up to the superior numbers and were continually having to shield their exposed sides that formed a target for the enemy... In the end they were all driven into a mass and fought from behind a *testudo*, as though they were in a siege. Bombarded from every side, they held out bravely for as long as they could, but finally they were all destroyed. This terrible disaster, which no one cares to recall, was a setback to the Romans, since a vast army, matching anything in earlier generations for courage and endurance, had been destroyed (Her. 6.5.9–10).

The Romans had been lulled into a false sense of security because their advance had so far encountered no opposition, but above all they believed that the emperor's main army had advanced and was no doubt trouncing Ardashir even as they moved on his defenceless capital. Evidently advancing without scouts, and not in a marching order that could readily form a line of battle, the Romans paid the ultimate price.

EPILOGUE

When the armies of the rival emperors Licinius and Maximinus Daia met in battle near Adrianople in AD 313, it was one of the last great encounters of legionary armies organized in cohorts and centuries. The armies advanced, centurions and standard-bearers leading the centuries, and came within missile range; but Daia's soldiers had already been unnerved by the sight of Licinius' army at prayer, and believed that their enemies were divinely inspired. The Licinians suddenly charged and, like Caesar's soldiers in the battle against Ariovistus, Daia's legionaries had no time to throw their javelins. As they struggled to draw their swords the Licinians were upon them, cutting down the leading ranks. At length Daia's men gave way, losing half their number (Lact. *DMP* 46–47). Lactantius' account of the battle is unfortunately brief and concerned mostly with the apparent inspiration of Licinius' men by the Christian god; but the elements of the old aggressive tactics are clear.

After this the tactics of the Romans became more defensive in all situations, the running charge being dropped in favour of a static shield wall, and the devastating combination of *pilum* and *gladius* giving way to other weapons. But when led by an old-style commander the regiments of the Late Empire could still be inspired to fight in the old way. In AD 363, on the plain before Ctesiphon, a Sassanian Persian army awaited the advance of Roman infantry led by the emperor Julian 'the Apostate' – a pagan in what was by then a Christian empire.

Maximinus (r.AD 235–238) was so called because he began his career as a common cavalryman but was promoted to the highest military commands – the name means something like 'Greatest–Smallest'. He was the first emperor recorded as having fought in battle in person while holding the throne; his features present a striking contrast to those of Severus Alexander, and the soldiers revered him as one of their own. After taking power he crossed the Rhine, and during the ensuing campaign he found his battle line hesitant to follow the Alamanni, who were withdrawing into a marsh. 'Maximinus plunged into the marsh on horseback (even though the water... came over the horse's belly), and killed many of the barbarians who resisted'; this example shamed his troops back into action (Her. 7.2.6-7). Despite his courage and military charisma, Maximinus too would soon fall victim to the chronic instability of the 3rd century empire. (Author's photo)

Following their emperor, the Roman infantrymen advanced slowly at first, swinging their shields as they came, as if to hypnotize the Persians. The Romans' helmets were crested and their armour polished, recalling the way that Lucullus' and Caesar's men went into battle in their finery. As they came within missile range the warcry was sounded and, like the legionaries of Lucullus and Ventidius, they charged at the run, getting inside the reach of the Persian arrows. The light infantry stung the Persians with javelins, the heavy infantry stabbed and hacked their way into the leading ranks of cataphracts with spears and swords. Julian cheered them on, and they barged their way through the overwhelmed cavalry and into the infantry beyond. The Persian infantry fell back, at first slowly, then turning to flight. The war elephants bringing up the rear of the Persian army did not come into action, probably having already turned back to the city. The Romans followed, slashing at the backs and legs of the fugitives.

The city gates were open to admit the fleeing Persians, but as the Romans were about to enter the city the newly cautious and defensive mentality asserted itself. A general, ironically named Victor, sounded the recall, and threw away the best opportunity the army had to take the Persian capital. His intentions were good: his soldiers might have been cut off and surrounded in the narrow streets and slaughtered piecemeal (Amm. Marc. 24.6–8–13). But Julian's army did not have the numbers to properly besiege such a great city, and what followed was a disaster. The Romans were forced to retreat, Julian was mortally wounded in a skirmish, and only a shattered remnant of the army that had almost carried Ctesiphon made it home.

Early 2nd-century AD legionaries and auxiliaries, including slingers and stone-throwers, assault a Dacian fort in a scene from Trajan's Column. Note, left, a standard-bearer, and auxiliary soldiers with scaling ladders. The former has a small, round shield of a type associated with standard-bearers, presumably to make it easy to sling and less awkward when handling the heavy standards. (RHC Archive)

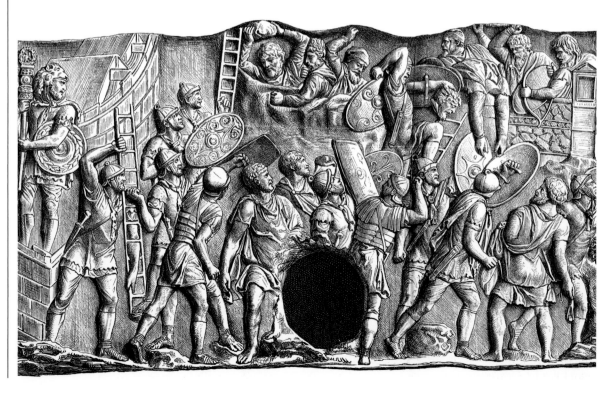

REFERENCES AND FURTHER READING

M.J.V.Bell, 'Tactical Reform in the Roman Republican Army', *Historia* 14 (1965), 404–422

A.Hyland, *Training the Roman Cavalry: From Arrian's* Ars Tactica (London, 1993)

B.Isaac, 'Hierarchy and Command-Structure in the Roman Army' in Y.Le Bohec (ed.), *Le hiérarchie (Rangordnung) de l'armée romaine sous le Haut-Empire* (Paris, 1995), 23–31

L.Keppie, *The Making of the Roman Army: From Republic to Empire* (rev. ed., London, 1998)

J.Kromayer & G.Veith, *Heerwesen und Kriegführung der Griechen und Römer* (Munich, 1928)

F.Lammert, 'Der Keil in der Taktik des Altertums', *Gymnasium* 51 (1940), 15–31

J.F.Lendon, *Soldiers and Ghosts: A History of Battle in Classical Antiquity* (New Haven & London, 2005)

P.Rance, 'The *Fulcum*, the Late Roman and Byzantine *Testudo*: The Germanization of Roman Infantry Tactics?', *Greek, Roman and Byzantine Studies* 44 (2004), 265–326

T.Rice Holmes, *Caesar's Conquest of Gaul* (2nd ed., Oxford, 1911)

M.P.Speidel, *The Framework of an Imperial Legion* (Cardiff, 1992)

G.Veith, *Geschichte der Feldzüge C. Julius Caesars* (Vienna, 1906)

G.Veith, 'Die Taktik der Kohortenlegion,' *Klio* 7 (1907), 303–334

E.L.Wheeler, 'The Legion as Phalanx', *Chiron* 9 (1978), 303–318

E.L.Wheeler, 'Battles and Frontiers', *Journal of Roman Archaeology* 11 (1998), 644–651

E.L.Wheeler, 'The Legion as Phalanx in the Late Empire (I)' in Y.Le Bohec & C.Wolff (eds), *L'Armée romaine de Dioclétien à Valentinien Ier* (Paris, 2004), 309–358

PLATE COMMENTARIES

A: LEGIONARY CENTURIES IN CLOSE AND OPEN ORDER

Two legionary centuries, one *prior* (front) and one *posterior* (rear), are depicted in close and open order respectively. The *prior* century is formed in eight ranks and ten files, each legionary occupying a space 3ft wide and probably 3ft deep (0.91m square). This spacing is given by Polybius in his account of the manipular legion, and appears to have remained standard into the Late Roman period (Polyb. 18.30.6). The number of soldiers in a *contubernium* (tent or mess group) was eight, and scholars have suggested that the *contubernium* also formed a file in the battle line, but there is no ancient evidence to confirm this. In the battle formation that Arrian drew up against the Alani (AD 135), the legionaries did form eight ranks. However, when on the march Arrian's legionaries marched four abreast, so his battle line may have been formed by *posterior* centuries drawn up immediately behind *prior* centuries, each century formed in four ranks and 20 files.

The *posterior* century is depicted in open formation, the legionaries drawn up in four ranks and 20 staggered files. Again following Polybius (18.30.7), in this open formation each soldier occupies a space 6ft by 6ft (1.83m square). The number of ranks is also suggested by Arrian's formation against the Alani; while there is no direct evidence for such a chessboard formation, it has long been favoured by scholars because it would allow more soldiers to use their weapons.

In both centuries the 'command group' of centurion, standard-bearer and trumpeter (*centurio, signifer, cornicen*) – here keyed **C, S & Tr** – are located in the centre of the first and second ranks. Most reconstructions place the centurion at the right of the front rank; but we know that in Late Roman cavalry units the commander, standard-bearer and trumpeter were grouped together at the front centre (*Strategicon* 3.2–4), and this arrangement also seems sensible for the century. To the rear of the century are postioned the *optio* – here keyed **O** – the centurion's second-in-command; and the *tesserarius* – **T** – the 'holder of the watchword'. Polybius tells us that the *optio's* place was in the rear, and the long staff with which he is often depicted suggests that he would shove soldiers back into rank (cf *Strategicon* 12.B.17; Speidel 1992, 24–26). *Tesserarii* are depicted with a similar long staff, and presumably aided the *optio* at the rear of the century when in battle.

59

TOP **Legionary helmet lost in the River Po during one of the battles of Cremona, AD 69. This rather crudely made bronze piece, now in the Museo Stibbert in Florence, was classified by H.Russell Robinson as Imperial Italic Type C. (Stephen D.P.Richardson)**

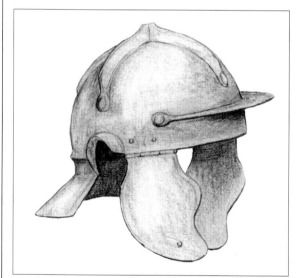

MIDDLE **Suggested reconstruction by Robinson, from sculptural and fragmentary archaeological sources, of a 2nd century AD bronze auxiliary helmet, classified as Auxiliary Infantry Type C. (Stephen D.P.Richardson)**

BOTTOM **Bronze legionary helmet contemporary with the battle of Issus (AD 194). This piece, marked to L.Sollonius Super of *legio XXX Ulpia Victrix* and found at Niedermörmter in Germany, is the latest currently known example of the development of the so-called Imperial Gallic and Italic types. Classified by Robinson as Imperial Italic Type H, it is now in the Rheinisches Landesmuseum, Bonn. (Steven D.P.Richardson)**

B: THE *TESTUDO*

The *testudo* ('tortoise') is famous for its use in siege warfare, but it was also widely employed in field battles, because it offered excellent protection against missiles. Here (**1** & **2**) we see part of the *testudo* formed by Mark Antony against horse archers during his retreat from Parthia in 36 BC. Antony's *testudo* appears to have been different from other such formations, in that all his legionaries knelt down; the first rank formed the shield wall, and the second and third ranks lifted their shields to create the forward-sloping roof (**2**). When the Parthians saw that the complete Roman army had halted its march and was kneeling down, they believed that the Romans had become too dejected to fight. The *testudo* formation protected them from the horse archers' arrows, so the Parthians gave up their hit-and-run tactics, took up their lances and attacked the formation at close quarters. This was exactly what Antony wanted: as soon as the Parthians came near, the legionaries leapt out of formation (**1, centre**) and finally got to grips with them (Plut. *Ant.* 45).

At (**3**) we show a file in a *fulcum*, a late Roman variant of the *testudo* that was much used as a defence against enemy cavalry (*Strategicon* 12.B.16; Rance 2004).

C: THE *CUNEUS* AND 'PIG'S HEAD'

Cuneus means 'wedge', but there is no evidence that the Romans used literally triangular-shaped infantry formations. *Cuneus* was a term applied to formations of various shapes – even squares or rectangular columns – in which the soldiers were formed in extremely close order (probably spaced 1.5ft by 1.5ft), and were employed to create or exploit gaps in enemy battle lines. One *cuneus* tactic may have been to advance two columns of infantry at converging angles so that they would strike the enemy at approximately the same point – a similar tactic had been advocated for the Macedonian phalanx, called the *embolon* (e.g. Asclep. Tact. 11.5). Here we see such a tactic employed by two legionary cohorts against rebel troops drawn up in poor order. Even before the heads of the columns strike, the portion of the rebel line facing the advance of the *cuneus* begins to panic and flee. The legionaries in the columns are drawn up six abreast, as suggested by Josephus' description of Vespasian's marching order in Judaea in AD 67 (Jos. *BJ* 3.124).

The **insets** shows a cohort of six centuries drawn up in three hypothetical interpretations of 'pig's head' formations. The pig's head was closely associated with the *cuneus*, and is vaguely described as being narrower at the front than it was at the back; the 'snout' of the formation was presumably flat.

D/E: BATTLE ARRAY

This reconstruction is based on the formation with which *legio III Augusta* and auxiliaries defeated the African rebel Tacfarinas in AD 17 (Tac. *Ann.* 2.52). The *triplex acies* (triple line) legionary formation was employed widely in the closing years of the Republic and presumably continued in use during the early Imperial period.

Here we see a legion (**centre**) of 60 centuries and ten cohorts drawn up in *triplex acies* using a 4-3-3 arrangement. The first line consists of 24 close-order centuries (four cohorts); the second and third lines each have 18 centuries (three cohorts). At some time in the 1st century AD the first cohort, positioned at the right of the first line (near left, as viewed here) was increased in size over the other nine, to five double-size centuries.

Reconstructions of the *triplex acies* often show the six centuries in each cohort formed up very close together, and with large intervals between adjacent cohorts. Here, by contrast, we show the centuries separated by an interval equalling the frontage of a century. This allows the first line of the legion to attack the enemy as a mass of small *cunei*, and if their charge is unsuccessful, the centuries of the second line can move forward to replace the leading centuries, or to fill the intervals between them. The third line of the legion is held as a reserve.

The legate (legion commander), his *vexillum* standard and his six tribunes are positioned behind the first cohort, with trumpeters to sound tactical signals (**inset 1**); from here he can direct the action, and send his tribunes with orders to the various components of the army. The 120 legionary cavalry behind him (**inset 2**) serve both as a bodyguard and a reserve (Jos. *BJ* 3.120). We speculate that the legion's *aquilifer* standard-bearer and its *primus pilus* – the senior centurion of the first cohort, a soldier of great prestige and authority – would be stationed in the front rank of that cohort (**inset 3**).

The legion is supported on each flank by two cohorts of auxiliary light infantry, with c.480 soldiers per cohort. The cohorts are in open order, appropriate to missile troops and skirmishers, with *posterior* centuries formed up behind the *prior* centuries. The second cohort on each flank is a

reserve. Our placing of a command group for each cohort beside its right front is speculative; we know that auxiliary cohorts – unlike legionary cohorts – had commanders and standards at this level, but not where they took position in battle. We have placed the auxiliary centurions and standard-bearers of the centuries in their front ranks (**inset 4**).

On each flank an *ala* of auxiliary cavalry, c.500 strong in 16 *turmae* or troops, completes the battle array; we have placed the commander, his *vexillarius* standard-bearer and *tubicen* trumpeter in the front ranks of the right hand *turma*; (**inset 5**) shows the command group of a European unit, Gallic or Thracian, and (**inset 6**) troopers of a Numidian unit.

While the legionaries (**inset 7**) make a frontal assault, the light infantry will add missile support; the cavalry will attempt to knock out the light troops and cavalry of the enemy army, preventing any envelopment by enemy flanking attacks, and will then swing inwards to assault the enemy main body from the flanks and rear.

Cornicen (trumpeter) and mail-clad *signifer* (standard-bearer), depicted on the Great Ludovisi battle sarcophagus, c.AD 260; the helmets depicted (lower right) are of so-called Attic type, of which some highly decorative examples have been found. The armour and equipment of the legionary still echoed those of the great reigns of the previous century, and occasional victories were still won in the old style. However, during the usually brief reigns of some 24 emperors between the mid-230s and mid-280s, all Rome's external enemies took advantage of the never-ending rebellions and civil wars which chronically weakened the empire's defences. (Author's photo)

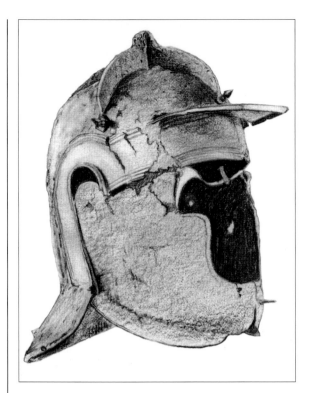

ABOVE **Helmets of this general type – with a very deep rear extension, large face-guards, a deep, pointed 'peak', and crossed reinforces over the skull – were classified by Robinson as Auxiliary Cavalry Type E and dated to the 2nd century. More recently, however, comparison with the scarce sculptural evidence has suggested that they were used by legionary infantry in the 3rd century AD (e.g. the gravestone of Julius Aufidius of *legio XVI Flavia Firma* at Veria). Changes in the design of military equipment normally respond to practical needs; we may speculate about the apparent need for more fully protective helmets in this period. This example, from Heddernheim and now in the Frankfurt Museum, is of iron with bronze fittings. (Steven D.P.Richardson)**

F: LEGIONARY CENTURY CHARGING

In the previous plate the legion's centuries were arrayed so as to form a row of *cunei* with the potential to puncture an opposing battle line. Here we see a late Republican or early Imperial century making a furious charge against the enemy. The leading two ranks have thrown their *pila* and sprint towards the enemy; the Roman soldier attempted to topple his opponents (Tac. *Hist*. 2.42), so speed was essential, and we can see here how the shield was used as a battering ram. Behind the sprinting swordsmen, the legionaries in ranks three and four have paused momentarily to hurl their *pila* over the heads of the leading ranks and into the enemy. The remaining four ranks follow up at an easy jog; while the preceding ranks have opened up, these legionaries retain good close order. As was typical in battles of the Republic, and presumably also the Empire, they drum their *pila* against their shields, and

BELOW LEFT **The legionary's deadly tool for close-quarter combat: a *gladius* of the late 1st century BC or early 1st century AD. This example belonged to a centurion, who had the hilt plated in silver. Personal displays of relative wealth by the decoration of weapons and other items seem to have been popular among Roman soldiers. (Steven D.P.Richardson)**

BELOW RIGHT ***Gladius* from Pompeii, c.AD 79, still in its scabbard. This type, with its parallel edges and shorter 'clipped' point, was the standard infantry sword from the mid 1st to mid 2nd centuries AD, and its shape suggests a weapon equally useful for both the cut and the thrust. (Steven D.P.Richardson)**

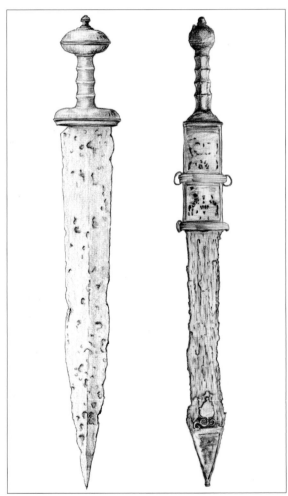

sing a paean to the war god Mars; the Romans believed that this gave the troops confidence and intimidated the enemy. The legionaries in the rear ranks do not throw their *pila* because of the risk of hitting their comrades in the leading ranks.

The dust and hazy atmosphere is typical of Roman battles, which were usually fought in the summer months, so the volume of dust raised by thousands of feet and hooves was immense. At the battle of Vercellae (101 BC) there was so much dust that for a time the Romans could not see the huge army of the Cimbri, and when some Roman units advanced into the dust cloud they unwittingly marched past the enemy (Plut. *Mar*. 26.3).

G: *LANCIARII* ATTACK PARTHIAN CATAPHRACTS

Here we see a century of *lanciarii* (**inset 1**) – light-armed legionaries equipped with *lanceae* – deploying from the interval between two centuries of heavy legionary infantry (**inset 2**), to swarm around a squadron of Parthian cataphracts in a battle of the 3rd century AD. Fooled by the tempting gap between the centuries of heavy infantry, the cataphracts – fully armoured cavalry (**inset 3**) – have charged on to a line of caltrops, leg-breaking pits and other booby-traps hidden in the sandy grassland before the Roman battle line. As the *lanciarii* bombard the stricken cavalry with their light javelins, another Parthian squadron wheels away before it hits the booby-traps.

Similar tactics were successfully employed by the Romans against the Parthians at the epic three-day battle of Nisibis in AD 217 (Her. 4.15.1–4). *Lanciarii* belonging to *legio II Parthica* fought at this battle, but their exact function is debated. Here they are presented as skirmishers, like the *velites* of the manipular legion; but some suggest that the *lanciarii* were positioned to the rear of the battle line, hurling their javelins over a heavy infantry shield wall (cf the rear four ranks of Arrian's legionary formation against the Alani).

H: CAVALRY WEDGE & *TESTUDO*

Triangular wedge and rhomboid cavalry formations had been employed by the ancient Greeks and Macedonians. The 2nd-century AD Roman general Arrian commends the wedge in his *Tactical Handbook*, but it remains unclear if the formation was actually used by Roman cavalry (Arr. *Tact*. 16). This plate presents at (**1**) a 3rd-century *turma* of 30 *contarii* (lancers) in a hypothetical wedge or *cuneus* of three ranks. The decurion (**1D**), commander of the *turma*, forms the point, and the *draconarius* standard-bearer (**1S**) rides in the rank behind him. Other under-officers, including a trumpeter (cf *Strategicon* 3.2), were probably concentrated in the leading ranks, so that 'all of the leaders fall on the enemy together.' Behind the *turma* the decurion's servant – *calo*, often a slave (**1C**) – follows on one of the decurion's remounts and leads the other on a long rein; officers and under-officers went into battle with spare horses. The servant also carries a spare *contus* (lance) for the decurion.

At (**2**) we show another variation of the *testudo*, here a loose shield wall formed by 3rd-century cavalrymen, who have formed up in a slightly oblique rank, with the horses' heads turned in, so as to present their shielded side to the enemy. The oblique line means that each trooper's shield also offers some protection to the head of the horse of the next rider (Arr. *Tact*. 36.1).

Funerary portrait of a legionary of the early 4th century AD; the long-sleeved tunic, long trousers, sword slung to the left hip, oval shield and multiple javelins are typical. (Steven D.P.Richardson)

INDEX

Figures in **bold** refer to illustrations.